Cooking Entrees With the Micheff Sisters

A Vegan Vegetarian Cookbook

Edited by Aileen Andres Sox
Designed by Michelle C. Petz
Front cover and interior photos: Mark Mosrie
Cover recipe: Veggie-Chicken Roll, p. 70

Additional copies of this book are available from two locations:
3ABN: Call 1-800-752-3226 or visit www.3abn.org
Adventist Book Centers: Call 1-800-765-6955
or visit www.adventistbookcenter.com

Library of Congress Cataloging-in-Publication Data

Johnson, Linda Micheff,
Cooking entrees with the Micheff sisters: a vegan vegetarian cookbook/Linda Micheff Johnson,
Brenda Micheff Walsh, Cinda Micheff Sanner.
p. cm.
ISBN: 0-8163-2135-3
ISBN 13: 9780816321353
1. Vegetarian cookery. 2.Vegan cookery. 3. Entrées (Cookery) I. Walsh, Brenda Micheff,
II. Sanner, Cinda Micheff, III. Micheff Sisters. IV. Title.

TX837.J542 2006
641.5'636—dc22
2005058655

06 07 08 09 10 • 5 4 3 2 1

Cooking Entrees With the Micheff Sisters

A Vegan Vegetarian Cookbook

3ABN BOOKS

P.O. Box 220 West Frankfort, Illinois

www.3ABN.org

Pacific Press® Publishing Association

Nampa, Idaho

Oshawa, Ontario, Canada

www.PacificPress.com

Foreword

You've heard it said, "The way to a man's heart is through his stomach." But, it's not just a man's heart that is wooed and won by good food, it's also the hearts of children, family members, and friends—and the occasional stranger that might grace your table. And men, if you want to put sparkle back into your wife's eyes, just surprise her with some culinary delight you've lovingly prepared for her! Family counselors agree there's no better way to create great memories than to combine family fun, laughter, and stimulating conversation with the enjoyment of the mouth-watering aromas and taste of great food!

That's why I'm so excited about the Micheff sisters' entree cookbook of more than a hundred totally vegetarian entrees. What a gift they have given to us. With these simple-to-follow recipes you don't need to slave away all day over the stove, mixing, grinding, blending, pureeing, and simmering exotic ingredients in order to create memory-making meals. In fact, there's a whole section of one-dish recipes which are perfect for busy, overcommitted twenty-first century families. The sisters have made the art of gourmet cooking easy—and healthy! Everyone can do it—even I can!

The food and friendship of the Micheff sisters—Linda, Brenda, and Cinda—have not only enriched my life—but the lives of millions of others who have grown to love them through their television ministry on 3ABN. Not only do they volunteer their time to produce 3ABN's children's programming, *Kids Time, Kids Time Praise,* and *Tiny Tots for Jesus,* but they combine their humor and wholesome camaraderie on 3ABN's cooking segments as they encourage and teach viewers all over the world how to prepare totally vegetarian meals. You'll grow to love them as they share with you the cooking tips that they've used since they were growing up together under the guidance of their mom, Bernie Micheff.

The entrees in this cookbook are destined to become family favorites. Why not start creating memories today as you mix together love and laughter, with the wonderful taste of the Micheff sisters' award-winning recipes.

Kay Kuzma,
Friend
President, Family Matters Ministry

Tribute to Our Children

One of the greatest gifts God has ever given to woman is the gift of children.
This gift has helped us to better understand God's amazing love.
We treasure this precious gift and because we love our children with all our hearts;
we are dedicating our second cookbook to them.

To Jimmy (Linda's son): Some of my most precious memories with you were cooking together in the kitchen. I loved spending time with you preparing our meals. You loved to help make pancakes shaped like animals and smiley face cookies and mashed potato mountains with gravy. Now that you have a home of your own I see you doing some of the same special things with your family.
I am so proud of you and just want you to know how very much

I love you, Mom.

To Becky and Linda Kay (Brenda's girls): The memories that are dearest to my heart are the times that we have shared together at home. I loved it when you would invite your friends over and we would all end up in the kitchen together making cookies, apple pie, or homemade pizza.
Or the times when it would be just "us girls" fixing some of our family favorites.
Then we would sit around the table sharing the days' events or things that were on our hearts.
I can't begin to tell you how precious those times were to me. I am so very proud of both of you and the beautiful women that you are today and I still love those special moments with you!
There are not enough words to express the love in my heart for you.

I love you dearly, Mom.

To David and Catie (Cinda's children): From the time you both were little I knew that being your mom was the most important thing in the whole world. I treasured every moment with you. But some of my favorite bonding times with you both were in the kitchen. From the time you were old enough to sit on the counter, I had you helping me with the mixing and stirring and adding of ingredients. There would always be flour from one end of the kitchen to the other when we were finished—but the messes didn't bother me at all. It was the laughter and fun that we shared together that meant so much to me. Now that you are grown and pretty much on your own I cherish those precious memories. I am so proud of both of you and I just want you to know that

I love you with all my heart, Mom.

Psalm 127:3, reminds us that "Children are a heritage of the Lord."
We thank the Lord for each one of you.

Acknowledgments

We would like to express our heartfelt thanks to all those who helped make
Cooking Entrees With the Micheff Sisters possible.

We appreciate Three Angels Broadcasting Network and their worldwide ministry in promoting Bible truths and the health message. We are thankful to 3ABN for letting us have a small part in sharing with others the abundant lifestyle that God offers.

We particularly want to thank our husbands for their willingness to taste our endless recipes. Their honest opinions and ideas make them great food critics. But most of all we want to thank Jim, Tim, and Joel for their unselfish love and their support. We love you guys!

We want to thank our precious parents for their unfailing love, listening ears, constant prayers, and for always being there for us. But most of all, thank you for making Jesus the center of our home and inspiring us to share God's love with others. Mom and Dad, we love you with all our hearts!

We want to thank our special friend Kay Kuzma for her encouragement in all the ministries we are involved in. Her love for Jesus is contagious! We love you, Kay!

We also want to thank Pacific Press, our publisher, for their many hours of hard work to make this cookbook possible: Susan Harvey, for her vision and enthusiasm; Tim Lale, for his many hours of hard work, support, and direction; Aileen Andres Sox, for her countless hours editing the recipes; and Michelle Petz for doing such a beautiful job on our cookbook's design and cover.

Most of all we want to thank our awesome God for His many blessings and unconditional love for each one of us. We love You, Jesus, and we are looking forward to spending eternity with You!

Table of Contents

Introduction

From the time we were little we loved "assisting" Mom in the kitchen. What fun we had helping her make scrumptious meals! We would laugh and tease each other while shaping our bread dough into rolls, making cookies and other goodies to surprise Daddy with. We could hardly wait for him to come home so we could give him the food we had made. After the meal was prepared we would help set the table for our special time together. Someone had given Mom some blue goblets that didn't seem to fit in with our chipped dishes and mismatched silverware. But we thought our table was beautiful!

When Daddy came home, there was great excitement as we all gathered around the table anxious to hear about his witnessing experiences throughout the day. Mom would bring out the casserole or entree and set it on the table. We would join hands and thank God for the good food and ask Him to bless our time together. Looking at our blue goblets and chipped dishes and our simple one-dish meals, we thought we were the richest family in the world! We have found that those times spent around the family table have drawn our hearts together in lasting bonds.

Now that we are grown, we still take pleasure in fixing special meals for our families. The smells of home-baked goodies coming from our ovens and food simmering on top of our stoves entice them to the kitchen. We still love making our tables special and inviting for our families.

Mom taught us that building a meal around a main dish helps take care of some of the stress that a fast-paced life offers. It is also more cost effective! We have put together a cookbook that is filled with recipes focused on entrees. We hope that this will make your meal-planning easier and your meals faster to prepare.

We encourage you not only to fix healthy food for your families but to invite them to help prepare the meals. Set your table like you would for guests and share your meal as a family around the table. The fellowship of sharing the day's events and the smells of good food will stay in the minds of your loved ones, and when they are grown, those memories will turn their hearts toward home.

We hope this cookbook will be a blessing for you and your families.

With God's Richest Blessings,
Linda, Brenda, and Cinda
The Micheff Sisters

Substitutions

Listed below are some of the substitutes we use in our recipes.

DAIRY SUBSTITUTES

Soy Good: This is a vegan soymilk that is one of our favorites. There are two kinds: plain and simple (which is good for soups and gravies and over breakfast cereals) and the regular classic vanilla Soy Good (it has a green label and is good for anything that requires a sweeter taste.) This does not have a strong aftertaste, which is one more reason that we love this milk!

Better Than Milk: This is also a favorite, and we like the original flavor best. This product is great to cook with and is great for cold cereals and any recipe that calls for milk. The vanilla flavor is good for cookies, cakes, and baked goods. This product is great because it too does not have an aftertaste like some soy products do! If you do not have either of our favorite soy milks, you can substitute your favorite brand.

Soy milk: All references to *soy milk* in our recipes refer to the plain flavored soy milk unless otherwise noted. Soy milk replaces regular milk cup for cup in any recipe.

Non-dairy whip topping: This is a substitute for whip cream but is a dairy free item that can be found in most of your local grocery stores and any natural food store. You can use any brand that you choose.

Tofutti Better Than Cream Cheese: This is similar in taste and texture to traditional cream cheese but is milk- and butterfat-free and contains no cholesterol. It comes in 8-ounce containers and is available in ten different flavors. It is great for making entrees or desserts, or just used as a spread for bagels. You can use this whenever a recipe calls for cream cheese.

Tofutti Sour Supreme: This product is our favorite. It looks and tastes pretty close to dairy sour cream but is milk- and butterfat-free and contains no cholesterol. This product can be used in any recipe that calls for sour cream. It is available in four flavors.

Soy cheese: We like the Tofutti brand best. It has no casein or animal products in it. It is a milk-free soy cheese. Flavor choices are Cheddar, American, or Monterey Jack.

Soy margarine: Look in your local grocery or natural food store and find a brand that is vegan and non-hydrogenated and has no trans fats or cholesterol.

NATURAL SWEETENERS

Florida Crystals: People always ask us, "What is pure Florida crystals?" Here is the answer: Pure Florida Crystals offers an excellent alternative to refined sugar. This product is an organic cane sugar milled on the day of harvest, with one simple crystallization. The juice is pressed from sun-ripened sugar cane, washed, filtered, and crystallized right on the farm. No additives or preservatives, nothing artificial—just natural sweetness, and absolutely no animal products used in the filtering process! Most white sugar that you purchase in your local grocery store is processed using bone char from animals in the filtering process. Florida Crystals replaces white refined sugar cup for cup.

Pure maple syrup: This is an all-natural product and is used in many recipes as a substitute for granulated sugar. It is less expensive if purchased at large membership stores. It is also available in most local grocery stores.

100% frozen fruit juices: We love these all-natural sweeteners. We use apple juice and white grape juice most frequently because its flavor does not overwhelm your recipe or change the color.

Sucanat by Wholesome Foods: This is an organic evaporated sugar cane juice with blackstrap molasses added to it. It replaces brown and white sugar cup for cup.

Evaporated cane juice crystals: This organic sugar is made from 100 % certified organic sugar cane. It is a "first crystallization" sugar, which means the cane is harvested, the juice is extracted, any field impurities are removed, and it is crystallized. All this is done within twenty-four hours of the harvest. Because it is far less processed than traditional white sugars, it retains a natural blond color and a delicious natural taste. It replaces white or brown sugar cup for cup.

TOFU

Tofu is an excellent source of protein and contains no cholesterol. It also is an inexpensive substitute for meat, fish, poultry, and cheese.

Silken tofu: This soybean product has a silky smooth texture, and is great for cheesecakes, pies, puddings, and salad dressings.

Water-packed tofu: This comes in soft, firm, or extra firm. It has to be refrigerated and has an earlier expiration date. The texture of even the soft tofu is a firmer, spongier texture, and it is great for things like mock scrambled eggs. It can be crumbled and will hold its shape, so it is very useful in all kinds of recipes. It can be blended until smooth or sliced or baked or boiled. The ideas are endless. It is a wonderful product.

Mori-Nu Tofu: These do not have to be refrigerated until opened and have a long shelf life. This is an excellent product and is great for making entrees, desserts, salad dressings, mock egg salad, and many other dishes.

Mori-Nu Mates: This is a substitute for pudding mix and it comes in lemon and vanilla flavors. These can be found in the health food section of your large grocery or natural food store.

MAYONNAISE

Grapeseed Oil Vegenaise: It is a great mayonnaise replacement. Grapeseed oil is an excellent natural source of vitamin E and essential fatty acids necessary for normal cell metabolism and maintenance. It is found only in the refrigerated sections of your grocery or natural food store and can be used cup for cup to replace any recipe asking for mayonnaise.

SEASONINGS

Liquid Aminos by Bragg: This is an unfermented soy sauce replacement. It is an all purpose seasoning made from soy protein. It can be used in entrees, in Oriental foods, to marinate, in gravies, and in any recipe that calls for soy sauce.

Vegex: This is a seasoning that comes in a paste. It is an extract of brewers yeast, and it is an all vegetable composition that has a beef flavor. You can use it in soups, stews, broths, gravies, or any recipe in which you desire a beefy taste. If you can't find this product, use a vegetarian beef bullion, which comes in dehydrated cubes, paste, or powder.

Nutritional yeast flakes: This is one of the most perfect foods known. It is a powerful health source of B-vitamins, amino acids, proteins, minerals, enzymes, and nucleic acids. This premium yeast is grown on sugar beets, which are known to absorb nutrients from the soil faster than almost any other crop. As a result, this yeast is exceptionally rich in selenium, chromium, potassium, copper, manganese, iron, zinc, and other factors natural to yeast. It is also gluten free. This yeast can be used in entrees or as a breading, sprinkled on top of foods like popcorn, or tofu scrambled eggs, and so many other ways!

McKay's vegan Chicken and Beef Style Seasoning: Dismat Corporation has been producing McKay's Chicken and Beef Broth and Seasonings for over sixty years. They use no meat or meat by-products in their seasonings. They do have products with MSG, so look carefully at the labels. There is NO MSG in their products labeled "vegan." They do not use hydrogenated shortening—only soy oil, and all their products are gluten-free!

OTHER PRODUCTS

Carob chips: These are a great alternative to chocolate chips. Some carob chips have dairy and lots of sweeteners in them. Be sure and look for the vegan ones sweetened with barley malt. These can be found in your local co-ops or health food stores or larger grocery stores.

Baking powder: We use Rumford's because it is an aluminum-free baking powder. You can use any aluminum-free baking powder of your choice.

Egg replacer: This is found in natural food stores. Cornstarch works just as well or better and costs a whole lot less. We use 1 tablespoon of cornstarch per egg. If you need the liquid from an egg, add an extra tablespoon of whatever liquid is in your recipe or just add a tablespoon of water.

Pecan meal: This is pecans that have been ground into a fine meal. This product can usually be found in your local grocery stores or purchased at the larger grocery stores, or you can make your own by grinding pecans in a food processor.

MEAT SUBSTITUTES

Dressler's Soy Add-ums: This is an unflavored dry textured soy protein made from defatted soy flour, which is the only ingredient, making it easier to digest without gassy aftereffects! When hydrated and flavored, it has the excellent "mouth feel" of a soft chewy meat with no aftertaste. This product takes on whatever flavor you add. It is inexpensive and can be used in any recipe that calls for beef or chicken. Some of our favorite recipes are Rosemary Chicken Potato Pizza, Walnut Chicken Stir Fry, and Vegetarian Fish Sticks, just to name a few!

Yves Ground Round Veggie Original: This is a soy protein product that is fat-free and cholesterol-free, and contains no preservatives. It is pre-cooked so all you do is heat and it is ready! This product can be used in any recipe that calls for ground hamburger meat, and of all the vegeburger products that we have tried, this one has a texture that most resembles real hamburger. (At least that is what we are told by meat eaters!) They also have a whole line of other products available that I love as well! Most of their products are NO fat or LOW fat! Try their Veggie Dogs. They taste delicious and are fat free!

Vibrant Life Foods: These products are specifically formulated to meet the highest standards of health and nutrition while emphasizing superior taste and texture. They provide a wide selection of natural foods—whole grains, flours, seeds, nuts, soy products—many of which are organically grown, without the use of chemical sprays or pesticides. Their meat substitutes, such as Vegeburger, vege-Franks, Vege-Scallops, etc., have an excellent flavor and texture, making them a perfect choice for a wide variety of recipes.

FLOUR

White wheat flour: This flour is made from white wheat berries that are triple-cleaned whole kernels of hard white wheat. It has all the nutrients that traditional red wheats have but is lighter in color and sweeter in taste. It does not contain the strongly flavored phenolic compounds found in red wheats, and because it is naturally sweet tasting, it requires less added sweeteners. It is golden in color and thus the name "white wheat."

RICE

Basmati brown rice (bahs-MAH-tee): This aromatic, long-grain rice is grown in the foothills of the Himalayas and is especially popular in India. The cooked grains are dry and fluffy, so they make a nice bed for curries and sauces. Basmati is available as either white or brown rice. Brown basmati has more fiber and a stronger flavor, but it takes twice as long to cook. Aged basmati rice is better, but more expensive. One cup dried rice yields three cups cooked rice.

Substitutes: popcorn rice (slightly milder than basmati) OR jasmine rice (has shorter grain than basmati, somewhat stickier; cooks slightly faster) OR long-grain rice (less expensive) OR wild pecan rice

Jasmine rice: Thai basmati rice = Thai jasmine rice. One cup dry rice yields three cups cooked rice. Jasmine rice is a long-grain rice produced in Thailand that's sometimes used as a cheap substitute for basmati rice. It has a subtle floral aroma. It's sold as both a brown and white rice.

Substitutes: basmati rice (Basmati rice has a longer grain, isn't as sticky, and takes slightly longer to cook.) OR popcorn rice OR patna rice OR other long-grain rice

Brown rice: whole grain rice. Many rice varieties come as either brown rice or white rice. Brown rice isn't milled as much as white, so it retains the bran and germ. That makes brown rice more fiber-rich, nutritious, and chewy. Unfortunately, it doesn't perform as well as white rice in many recipes. Long grains of brown rice aren't as fluffy and tender, and short grains aren't as sticky. Brown rice also takes about twice as long to cook and has a much shorter shelf life (because of the oil in the germ). Keep it in a cool, dark place for not more than three months. Refrigeration can extend shelf life.

Substitutes: converted rice (less chewy, takes less time to cook) OR wild pecan rice OR white rice (Enriched white rich has less fiber, but many of the same nutrients.)

Risotto rice: Piedmont rice. This plump white rice can absorb lots of water without getting mushy, so it's perfect for making risotto. The best comes from Italy. Arborio is very well-regarded, but Carnaroli, Roma, Baldo, Padano, and vialone nano (= nano) are also good. The highest Italian risotto rice grade is superfino. Lesser grades are (in descending order) fino, semi-fino, and commune. You can sometimes find brown risotto rice, which has more fiber and nutrients, but it isn't nearly as creamy as white risotto rice. Never rinse risotto rice—you'll wash off the starch that gives it such a creamy consistency.

Substitutes: granza rice (shorter grain, works fine in risottos or paellas) OR short-grain white rice OR pearl barley (works well for risotto, but gives it a chewier texture) OR medium-grain white rice (may make risotto mushy)

SEAWEED

Nori: Nori are thin, dried seaweed sheets. Nori sheets are used in many sushi dishes, for rice balls, and as a topping or condiment for various noodle and other dishes. It is also used in vegan vegetarian recipes whenever a "fishy" taste is needed for a particular dish.

This seaweed is high in fiber, protein, vitamins, and minerals. Compared with dairy products, seaweed provides up to ten times more calcium and iron by weight, and contains other important trace minerals. Seaweed has traditionally been eaten by people in Asian cultures to strengthen the circulatory system and help lower cholesterol. Today scientists are researching other potential health benefits of seaweed.

Seaweed has anxiety-fighting properties, and it is packed with stress-relieving magnesium, as well as pantothenic acid and vitamin B2 (riboflavin).

Kelp: It is made from raw seaweed and is used in soups and stews, stir-fried with vegetables, or cooked with beans or grains. It cooks quickly and dissolves in longer-cooking dishes. It contains a natural glutamic acid, a tenderizer that helps beans cook quickly and makes them more digestible. It also contains alginic acid, a substance used as a thickening and stabilizing agent in food production. Kelp can be pre-soaked or added dry to foods with liquids. Kelp absorbs up to five times its weight in liquid.

Buying and storing tips: Dehydrated kelp should be stored in an airtight container in a dark, dry place. Cooked kelp should be kept refrigerated.

Availability: Kelp is sold dehydrated and in flake and powder forms for use as a condiment.

Beans & Grains

Black Bean Cakes and
Red Pepper Coulis
p. 21

Potato Corn
Tacos
p. 33

Raisin
Pecan Pilaf
p. 26

Santa Fe Rice Over Grilled Polenta
p. 24

Lentil Croquettes
p. 32

Home-Style Baked Beans

3 cups cooked Great
Northern beans

1 cup (8 ounces)
tomato sauce

1/4 cup pure maple
syrup

2 tablespoons apple-
juice concentrate

1 tablespoon Bragg
Liquid Aminos

1 teaspoon molasses

2 teaspoons lemon
juice

1 tablespoon McKay's
Beef Style
Seasoning

1 teaspoon onion
powder

1 tablespoon soy
margarine
(optional)

1 small onion, minced

2 tablespoons
imitation bacon
bits

Combine all ingredients in a large bowl. Spray a 1 1/2-quart baking dish with nonstick cooking spray. Pour the mixture into the baking dish. Bake at 350 degrees for 45 to 60 minutes. Serve hot or cold.

My husband loves these simple and quick homemade beans. I serve them with potato salad, whole-wheat buns, veggie burgers, and a colorful vegetable tray. I top off the meal with my homemade apple pie. This meal always puts a smile on his face and I love to see that smile! —Linda

Yield: 6 1/2-cup servings

Serving: Cal. 183   Fat 1.1g   Sat. fat <1g   Sod. 336.4mg   Carb. 35.6g   Diet. fiber 7.2g   Sugars 12.6g   Prot. 9.1g

Fiesta Black Beans & Brown Rice

Sauté onions in 1/2 cup water until water has evaporated. Add tomatoes, black beans, yellow peppers, salsa, salt, cumin, and garlic powder. Simmer 20 to 25 minutes on medium heat. Pour over hot steamed brown rice. Top with lettuce and tomatoes. Garnish with Tofutti Sour Supreme, black olives, and a sprig of cilantro.

For brown rice: Put rice in a 3-quart baking dish. Add salt and hot water. Cover with foil, shiny side down. Bake at 350 degrees for 45 to 60 minutes until rice is soft. Lift the foil off the rice carefully because the steam will be hot.

For variety omit the lettuce and tomato and serve the Fiesta Black Beans over fresh corn bread instead of the brown rice. Top each serving with a teaspoon or so of Tofutti Sour Supreme. Prepare a colorful leafy green vegetable salad to complete your meal and enjoy! —Linda

BROWN RICE

- 2 1/2 cups uncooked brown rice
- 2 teaspoons salt
- 5 cups hot water

- 1 cup finely chopped onions
- 1/2 cup water
- 3 cups canned diced tomatoes
- 3 1/4 cups cooked black beans
- 1/2 cup chopped yellow bell peppers
- 1/2 cup mild salsa
- 3/4 teaspoon salt
- 1 teaspoon cumin
- 1/4 teaspoon garlic powder
- 5 cups steamed brown rice (recipe below)
- 5 cups shredded lettuce
- 1 cup sliced grape tomatoes
- 1/2 cup Tofutti Sour Supreme
- 1/4 cup sliced black olives
- 1/4 cup chopped cilantro

Yield: 10 1/2-cup servings beans; 10 1/2-cup servings rice

Serving (beans): Cal. 257 Fat 3.5g Sat. fat 2.3g Sod. 756.1mg Carb. 48.6g Diet. fiber 8.8g Sugars 1.7g Prot. 9.6g
Serving (rice): Cal. 172 Fat 1.3g Sat. fat <1g Sod. 469.4mg Carb. 36.2g Diet. fiber 1.6g Sugars 0g Prot. 3.6g

Refried Beans

6 cups cooked pinto beans

1/4 cup taco sauce

2 tablespoons canola oil

1/3 cup flour

Combine pinto beans and taco sauce in a large mixing bowl. Mash beans with a potato masher or electric mixer until almost smooth. Small pieces of beans should still be visible.

In a large skillet heat oil and add flour until all oil is absorbed. Stir constantly over medium heat until flour mixture is golden brown.

Add pinto bean mixture to skillet with the browned flour. Mix well and cook on low for 3 to 5 minutes. Serve hot!

This dish is wonderful to serve with Spanish rice or any Mexican entree. I also use it for bean burritos. I cook the beans the night before or use canned beans to make preparation faster. You can make this dish ahead of time and heat just before serving. —Brenda

Yield: 13 1/2-cup servings

Serving: Cal. 128   Fat 3.1g   Sat. fat <1g   Sod. 358mg   Carb. 19.7g   Diet. fiber 5.2g   Sugars <1g   Prot. 5.8g

Potato & Baked Bean *Casserole*

Preheat oven to 400 degrees. Slice potatoes in 1/8-inch slices and parboil for 4 to 5 minutes. (They should still hold their shape and not be fully cooked.) Drain and lightly toss with olive oil. Set aside.

In a sauce pan over medium heat, melt margarine. Add onion and sauté until tender and clear. Add tomato sauce, lemon juice, cane juice crystals, and soy sauce. In a separate mixing bowl, stir together with a fork the apple-juice concentrate and cornstarch until smooth. Add to sauce mixture and bring to a boil. Turn down and let simmer for 5 minutes until thick.

Add all remaining ingredients. Pour into casserole baking dish, then layer top with potato slices, overlapping them slightly and completely covering the entire bean mixture. Cover with foil and bake for 40 minutes. Remove foil and bake for an additional 20 minutes until potatoes are golden and lightly browned. Serve hot!

For variety, try substituting different beans such as black beans, fava beans, etc. I love the combination of potatoes with the beans. It reminds me of traditional baked beans that you would serve with a potato salad! —Brenda

1 pound potatoes, peeled
2 tablespoons olive oil
1 tablespoon soy margarine
1 medium onion, minced
1 1/4 cups tomato sauce
1/3 cup lemon juice
1/4 cup evaporated cane juice crystals
1/4 cup soy sauce
1 cup apple-juice concentrate
1/4 cup cornstarch
1/4 cup ketchup
1 14-ounce can lima beans
1 14-ounce can Great Northern beans
1 14-ounce can garbanzo beans
1 14-ounce can pinto beans
1 teaspoon thyme
1 teaspoon marjoram

Yield: 14 1/2-cup servings

Serving: Cal. 255   Fat 4.1g   Sat. fat <1g   Sod. 695mg   Carb. 45.8g   Diet. fiber 8.9g   Sugars 5.8g   Prot. 10.4g

Black Bean Gluten Steaks

2 cups cooked black beans

1 medium onion, chopped

1/2 cup quick oats

1/2 cup nutritional yeast flakes

1 teaspoon garlic powder

1 teaspoon onion powder

1 teaspoon McKay's Vegan Beef Style Seasoning

1 teaspoon salt

1 1/2 cups cold water

1/4 cup olive oil

1/2 cup whole-wheat flour

2 cups gluten flour

Broth (recipe below)

BROTH

1 1/2 cups diced tomatoes

1 medium onion, diced

3/4 cup Bragg Liquid Aminos or soy sauce

2 tablespoons McKay's Vegan Beef Style Seasoning

12 cups water

Place the black beans, chopped onion, oats, nutritional yeast flakes, seasonings, cold water, and olive oil in a blender. Blend until smooth. Pour into a large bowl or a heavy duty mixer. Add the whole-wheat flour and gluten flour. Knead by hand or in the mixer until soft and smooth in texture. Form mixture into a long roll about 2 1/2 inches in diameter. Slice into 1/2-inch thick pieces. Pat gluten pieces into circles and drop into a large kettle or crock pot of boiling broth. Boil gently for 30 to 35 minutes. Reduce heat and continue cooking for 45 to 50 minutes. Let cool. Place in containers with a little of the broth, and store in the refrigerator or freezer until ready to use.

For broth: Mix ingredients together in a large kettle or crock pot and bring to a boil.

These Black Bean Gluten Steaks are good breaded and baked in the oven on a tray that has been greased with olive oil or sprayed with a nonstick cooking spray. Serve with sautéed onion and garnish with fresh parsley and sliced grape tomatoes. They also can be put on a whole-wheat bun with lettuce, tomato, onion, or baked in the oven in your favorite sauce. —Linda

Yield: 40 3-inch steaks

Per steak: Cal. 81   Fat 1.9g   Sat. fat <1g   Sod. 182.2mg   Carb. 8.7g   Diet. fiber 2.3g   Sugars <1g   Prot. 8.6g

Black Bean Cakes & Red Pepper Coulis

In a medium skillet over medium-high heat, sauté the carrot and onion in oil until the onion is clear. Add the peppers and sauté 2 to 3 minutes until peppers are soft. Add the black beans, and seasonings to the pan and mix well. Cook for an additional 5 minutes. Set aside to cool slightly. Transfer ingredients in skillet to a mixing bowl and add cornmeal until the mixture is sticky enough to form into patties. Pan fry patties in a small amount of oil or nonstick cooking spray, until browned and crispy. Serve warm with one tablespoon red pepper coulis on each cake.

For red pepper coulis: Mix all ingredients in blender and serve at room temperature over black bean cakes.

For those of you who may not have used the name, a coulis is a puree or thick sauce. You pronounce it koo-lee. You can freeze the uncooked patties between sheets of wax paper. Just make sure they are completely thawed out before frying. I make one-inch patties to serve as appetizers. Everyone loves them so make a lot. They'll disappear fast! —Cinda

1 cup shredded carrots

1 medium onion, minced

1/4 cup canola or olive oil

1 medium red bell pepper, minced

1 medium yellow bell pepper, minced

3 cups cooked & drained black beans

2 teaspoons cumin

1 tablespoon fresh or dried parsley

1/4 to 1/2 teaspoons cayenne pepper

1 1/2 teaspoons salt

1 cup cornmeal

Red pepper coulis (recipe below)

RED PEPPER COULIS

1 15-ounce jar roasted red peppers, drained

1/2 teaspoon minced fresh garlic

1 tablespoon extra-virgin olive oil

1 tablespoon vegetable stock

Salt to taste

Yield: 16 servings of 1 3-inch cake + 1 tablespoon coulis

Serving: Cal. 150   Fat 5.6g   Sat. fat <1g   Sod. 572.4mg   Carb. 21.1g   Diet. fiber 4.9g   Sugars 1.2g   Prot. 4.8g

Lentil Stew

2 cups dry lentils

8 cups water

1/2 teaspoon garlic powder

1 tablespoon salt

1 tablespoon McKay's Vegan Chicken Style Seasoning

2 tablespoons McKay's Vegan Beef Style Seasoning

4 cups canned diced tomatoes

1 cup mild salsa

1 medium onion

2 cups carrots

1 cup Dressler's Soy Add-ums

Steamed brown rice (recipe on p. 17)

Wash the lentils and put them into a large kettle. Add the rest of the ingredients. Bring to a boil and reduce heat. Boil gently 45 to 60 minutes until lentils are soft. Serve over brown rice.

This stew is also good served over whole-wheat toast, topped with shredded lettuce and chopped tomatoes and a tofu ranch dressing. Garnish with sliced black olives. —Linda

Yield: 20 1/2-cup servings

Serving: Cal. 125   Fat 1.1g   Sat. fat <1g   Sod. 815mg   Carb. 20.5g   Diet. fiber 4.5g   Sugars 4.5g   Prot. 11.1g

Costa Rican Black Beans

In a large stock pot over medium heat, add oil. Sauté celery, onion, pepper, tomatoes, garlic, and ginger until vegetables are tender and onion is clear. Add remaining ingredients except roux. Simmer for 30 minutes. Add roux and stir well. Bring back to a boil and simmer an additional 5 to 10 minutes. Serve hot over bowls of steaming rice.

For roux: Stir flour, oil, and vegetable stock together until well mixed.

My husband, Joel, our children, and I traveled to Costa Rica. We had black beans and rice for breakfast, lunch, and dinner! For breakfast the black beans and rice are mixed together. It is so common there that even the McDonald's fast food restaurants have it on their breakfast menus! Believe it or not, even after having it every day for two weeks, I still like it. I came home and created my version of it. You can add toppings such as diced tomatoes, avocado, and lettuce for variety. While you may not want to eat it three times a day, I think you will enjoy it for an occasional meal! —Cinda

ROUX
6 tablespoons flour
2 tablespoons oil
6 tablespoons vegetable stock

2 tablespoons canola or olive oil
1 cup minced celery
1 medium sweet onion, minced
1 medium red bell pepper, minced
1 cup chopped fresh tomatoes
1 teaspoon diced fresh garlic
1 teaspoon diced fresh ginger (optional)
3 cups cooked black beans or 4 15-ounce cans black beans, undrained
3 cups vegetable stock
1 teaspoon oregano
1 teaspoon cumin
3/4 teaspoon celery salt
3/4 teaspoon ground coriander seed
1/2 teaspoon thyme
1/2 teaspoon cayenne
1/4 teaspoon nutmeg
1/4 teaspoon clove
1/4 teaspoon allspice
Salt to taste
Roux (recipe at left)

Yield: 16 1/2-cup servings

Serving: Cal. 109   Fat 3.8g   Sat. fat <1g   Sod. 751.4mg   Carb. 15.2g   Diet. fiber 3.7g   Sugars 1.8g   Prot. 4.3g

Santa Fe Rice Over Grilled Polenta

1 tablespoon olive oil

1 medium onion, minced

1 teaspoon minced fresh or bottled garlic

2 cups cooked brown rice

2 cups cooked white rice

1 1/2 cups diced grape or Roma tomatoes

1 large red bell pepper, minced

2 small jalapeno peppers, diced

1/2 cup fresh lemon juice

1 1/2 teaspoons dried chervil

1/2 teaspoon dried basil

1 pound frozen sweet corn

1 15-ounce can black beans, drained

1 teaspoon salt

Grilled polenta (recipe at right)

2 cups shredded fresh spinach

Sour cream or ranch dressing (recipe on p. 116)

GRILLED POLENTA

1 1/2 cups cornmeal

3 cups warm water

1/2 teaspoon salt

In a large saucepan, sauté the onion in the oil until it is clear in color. Add the garlic and sauté for another minute. Stir in the rice and mix well. Sauté 2 to 3 minutes. Add the tomatoes, peppers, lemon juice, chervil, basil, corn, beans, and salt and sauté for another 3 to 4 minutes. Put the shredded fresh spinach onto a colorful platter. Arrange the polenta on top of the spinach. Spoon the rice mixture over the polenta. Make sure some of the polenta still shows. Drizzle with sour cream or ranch dressing.

For grilled polenta: In a medium saucepan, stir together the ingredients. Heat and stir while bringing to a boil. Turn the heat down and cook for 10 minutes, stirring occasionally, until polenta is the consistency of thick mush. Spread polenta into a 9 x 13-inch pan that has been sprayed with a nonstick cooking spray. Chill in the refrigerator for 1 to 2 hours until firm.

When chilled, cut polenta into 3-inch squares and place on a baking sheet that has been sprayed with a nonstick cooking spray. Spray the tops of the polenta squares with the nonstick cooking spray. Put oven on Broil setting. Broil the polenta squares until they are golden brown. Watch very closely as they can easily burn! It only takes a minute or so for them to get golden brown. As an alternative to broiling, you may bake the polenta squares at 400 degrees for 10 to15 minutes.

This colorful meal is filled with lots of vitamins and minerals. The deeper colored fruits and vegetables have the most nutrition. I try to prepare meals that include a wide variety of vegetables or fruits. For luncheons or more formal dinners make individual servings for each guest. —Cinda

Yield: 24 1/2-cup servings rice; 12 3-inch squares polenta

Serving (rice): Cal. 88   Fat 1.1g   Sat. fat <1g   Sod. 141mg   Carb. 17.5g   Diet. fiber 2.7g   Sugars 1.3g   Prot. 3.1g
Per polenta square: Cal. 109   Fat 1.7g   Sat. fat <1g   Sod. 99.2mg   Carb. 20.7g   Diet. fiber 2.7g   Sugars <1g   Prot. 2.8g

Vegetable Cashew Pilaf

Wash the basmati rice in cold water. Pour into a bowl and cover with water. Leave to soak for about 30 minutes.

In a large frying pan heat the oil and add all the spices. Sauté for 1 to 2 minutes over medium heat. Add the onion and sauté until clear. Stir in the carrots and cook for 3 to 4 minutes. Drain the rice thoroughly and add to the pan together with the peas, sweet corn, and cashews. Sauté for 3 to 4 minutes. Add water and the Liquid Aminos. Bring to a boil, cover and simmer for about 15 minutes over low heat until all the water is absorbed. Let stand covered for 10 minutes. Serve hot.

I had never tasted Indian food until I met my husband, Joel. It was a favorite of his and so he began introducing the different dishes to me until I grew to love it as much as he does! He also made sure that both of our children were introduced to it so that they would love it too. No matter where we travel in the world, he always manages to find an Indian restaurant. Now I try to come up with foods that are similar to the ones we have had in the many Indian restaurants we have visited over the years. I served this to him along with my sister Brenda's Lentil Croquets and he loved it! —Cinda

2 cups basmati rice

2 tablespoons canola or olive oil

1 1/2 teaspoons cumin

1 teaspoon curry powder

2 bay leaves

1 1/2 teaspoons cardamom

4 whole cloves

1 onion, minced

1 cup shredded carrots

2 cups frozen petite peas

2 cups frozen sweet corn

1 1/2 cups whole cashews, roasted in microwave or sautéed in pan

4 cups water

1 tablespoon Bragg Liquid Aminos

Salt to taste

Yield: 22 1/2-cup servings

Serving: Cal. 167   Fat 6.3g   Sat. fat 1.2g   Sod. 81.3mg   Carb. 24.5g   Diet. fiber 2.6g   Sugars 2.8g   Prot. 4.5g

Raisin Pecan Pilaf

2 tablespoons canola oil

1 medium onion, minced

1 cup julienned carrots

1/2 cup raisins

3 cups frozen peas

1 teaspoon salt

1/2 teaspoon dried basil

3 cups cooked brown rice
(recipe on p. 17)

1 cup pecan halves, toasted

In a large nonstick skillet, add the canola oil. Stir-fry the onion, carrots, and raisins for 5 to 7 minutes until vegetables are slightly tender. Add the peas, salt, and basil. Cook 2 to 3 minutes. Add rice. Toast pecan halves in microwave or oven turning every 30 seconds until toasted. (Watch carefully since they tend to burn easily!) Add pecans to rice mixture. Serve hot!

This pilaf is good as a main dish or a side dish. Try adding grilled extra-firm tofu cut into bite-size chunks to this recipe; or add the tofu when sautéing the onion and vegetables. The raisins add a slight sweetness and the toasted pecans really top it off! —Brenda

Yield: 18 1/2-cup servings

Serving: Cal. 187 Fat 12g Sat. fat 1.1g Sod. 208mg Carb. 18.2g Diet. fiber 3.3g Sugars 1.2g Prot. 3.7g

Vegetable Fried Rice

Very good (handwritten)

Cut tofu into small pieces. Heat oil in large skillet and sauté with the onion until the onion is clear and the tofu is slightly browned. Add the carrots, snow peas, and broccoli and continue to sauté for 2 to 3 minutes until vegetables are slightly cooked. (You don't want them mushy!) Add the rest of the ingredients except the sesame oil and stir well. Sauté 4 to 5 minutes more. Add the sesame oil and mix well. Serve hot!

This is such a versatile dish! You can make it with your favorite vegetables. In the summertime I add zucchini and summer squash from my husband's garden. —Cinda

(handwritten): shredded carrots
baby frozen peas
yellow bell pepper 1/2
did 1/2 the amount →
(recipe)

- 1 12.3-ounce package Mori-Nu Extra-Firm Tofu
- 1 tablespoon canola or olive oil
- 1 small onion, minced
- 1 cup minced carrots
- 1 cup fresh snow peas cut in halves
- 1 cup chopped fresh broccoli (medium-sized pieces)
- 1 cup frozen petite peas
- 3/4 cup diced water chestnuts
- 2 teaspoons McKay's Vegan Chicken Style Seasoning
- 3 tablespoons Bragg Liquid Aminos
- 7 cups cooked medium-grain rice
- 1 tablespoon 100% pure dark sesame oil

Yield: 10 1/2-cup servings

Serving: Cal. 247 Fat 3.8g Sat. fat <1g Sod. 161.8mg Carb. 45.5g Diet. fiber 2.3g Sugars 2.8g Prot. 7.6g

Russian Rice-Filled Crepes

1 medium onion

1 tablespoon olive oil

1 cup grated carrots

1 tablespoon vegetable seasoning

3 cups cooked short-grain rice

Linda's Soy Crepes (recipe below)

LINDA'S SOY CREPES

1 cup whole-wheat pastry flour

1 cup unbleached white flour

1 teaspoon Rumford Baking Powder

1/2 teaspoon salt

1/3 cup soy milk powder

3 tablespoons unsweetened applesauce

3 cups water

Grate onion and sauté in olive oil. Add carrots and seasoning and sauté on medium heat until tender. Add rice. Stir together well and set aside. Place approximately 1/3 cup rice mixture in center of crepe. Fold envelope-style and place on platter. Serve warm or at room temperature.

For Linda's Soy Crepes: Combine all ingredients and beat well by hand or in blender. Let batter sit for about 10 minutes. Heat a 9-inch skillet to medium-high heat and spray with nonstick cooking spray. Pour 1/4 cup of batter into pan and immediately tilt and rotate pan so batter forms an even layer over the whole bottom. Cook over medium-high heat until the top starts to dry up and edges loosen. Slide pancake turner under the crepe, flip over, and cook the other side. Cool on wire rack.

My sisters and I had something very similar to this when we were in Russia at Pastor Valari's house. We loved it so much that his wife, Tatiana, gave us her recipe. We couldn't get most of the ingredients here in the United States so I did some experimenting and came up with this recipe that is very close to hers. These are good hot or room temperature, which makes them great to serve for a buffet. You can also fill Linda's crepes with any fruit filling and garnish with nondairy whipped topping and fresh fruit. —Brenda

Yield: 10 8-inch filled crepes

Serving (filling): Cal. 95 Fat 1.5g Sat. fat <1g Sod. 8.6mg Carb. 18.5g Diet. fiber <1g Sugars 1g Prot. 1.5g
Per crepe: Cal. 91 Fat <1g Sat. fat <1g Sod. 120.1mg Carb. 19.1g Diet. fiber 2g Sugars <1g Prot. 3.2g

Florentine Risotto

Thaw the frozen spinach and set aside, reserving the juice. In a blender or food processor, blend the tofu, 2 tablespoons of olive oil, salt, and 3 tablespoons of the spinach liquid until smooth and creamy. In a large saucepan over medium heat, sauté the onion in the remaining 1 tablespoon of olive oil until onion is clear. Add the rice and continue to sauté for 3 to 4 minutes. Mix the Chicken Style Seasoning into the 5 cups of water and add to the risotto mixture. Add the blended tofu and stir well. Cover the pan and simmer for 20 to 30 minutes or until liquid is absorbed. Mixture will be creamy and risotto will be al dente (soft, yet chewy). Serve hot.

Arborio rice grains are high in starch and shorter and fatter than any other short-grain rice. Arborio is used for risotto because its increased starch lends the dish its creamy texture. Regular grain rice will not give the creamy texture to this dish. You could also add sautéed mushrooms to this recipe.

If I want something extra special I bake this in tomato halves. Just spoon out the center of a medium-sized tomato and fill with the risotto. Place in a baking dish sprayed with a nonstick cooking spray. Bake at 350 degrees or until the tomato is tender and the risotto lightly browned. This recipe makes enough filling for 10 medium tomatoes. —Cinda

1 10-ounce package frozen diced spinach, thawed, save juice

1 12.3-ounce package Mori-Nu Silken Firm Tofu

2 tablespoons + 1 tablespoon olive oil

1 1/2 teaspoon salt

1 medium onion, diced

1 pound (2 1/2 cups) Arborio rice*

3 tablespoons McKay's Vegan Chicken Style Seasoning

5 cups water

Yield: 20 1/2-cup servings

Serving: Cal. 121   Fat 3.1g   Sat. fat <1g   Sod. 527.8mg   Carb. 24.3g   Diet. fiber 1g   Sugars <1g   Prot. 4.8g

Rice Patties

2 cups cooked small- or medium-grain rice

1/2 cup seasoned breadcrumbs

2 tablespoons soy margarine, melted

4 tablespoons soy sauce

1 12-ounce can vegetarian burger

Heat oven to 375 degrees. In a large mixing bowl mix all ingredients. If mixture is too dry, add a little water as needed. Mixture should not be wet but be able to hold together. Shape into patties and place on baking sheet, (sprayed with a nonstick cooking spray.) Bake for 30 minutes, remove from oven, and flip patties over. Return to oven for an additional 15 minutes. Patties should be crispy on the outside, tender on the inside. Serve hot or at room temperature.

These patties may also be fried in a skillet with olive oil if preferred. For variation add diced onion to the above ingredients and/or fresh minced garlic. My favorite vegeburger is Yves ground round because its texture most resembles hamburger. —Brenda

Yield: 14 3-inch patties

Per patty: Cal. 110 Fat 2g Sat. fat <1g Sod. 237.2mg Carb. 12.3g Diet. fiber 1g Sugars <1g Prot. 7.9g

Lentil Nut Roast

In a large mixing bowl combine all ingredients and mix well. Spray a 9 x 13-inch baking dish with a nonstick cooking spray and pour mixture into pan. Bake at 375 degrees for 1 hour. Top should be golden and crispy. Serve hot!

For variety try substituting different nuts, such as walnuts or almonds. This is also wonderful cold in sandwiches! —Brenda

2 cups cooked lentils

1 cup chopped pecans

1 1/2 cup soy milk

1/2 cup canola oil

1 teaspoon sage

2 cups crushed saltine crackers

1 cup Grape Nuts cereal

1 medium onion, minced or pureed

Yield: 12 1/2-cup servings

Serving: Cal. 344 Fat 24g Sat. fat 2.0g Sod. 317.4mg Carb. 28.3g Diet. fiber 5.7g Sugars 3g Prot. 7.9g

Lentil Croquettes

1 tablespoon olive oil
+ more for frying

1 medium onion,
minced

1 red bell pepper,
minced

3 garlic cloves,
crushed

1 cup cooked brown
lentils

1 teaspoon chili
powder

1 teaspoon cumin

2 teaspoons lemon
juice

1/2 cup crushed
peanuts

1 cup plain
breadcrumbs

Salt to taste

Spicy breadcrumbs
(recipe below)

SPICY
BREADCRUMBS

1 cup plain
breadcrumbs

2 teaspoons turmeric

2 teaspoons chili
powder

Heat 1 tablespoon olive oil in a skillet and sauté the onions until clear. Add the red pepper and garlic. Sauté until pepper is tender. Remove from heat and place in mixing bowl. Add all remaining ingredients except the spicy breadcrumbs. Shape mixture into oval croquettes, about 1 x 3 inches each. Roll croquettes in spicy breadcrumbs, coating completely. Heat olive oil in a large skillet. Add the croquettes in batches, and cook for about 10 minutes, turning once, until crispy on each side. Sprinkle with salt to taste. Serve hot!

For spicy breadcrumbs: In a large bowl, mix all ingredients together.

The croquettes should be crispy on the outside and soft and tender on the inside. They are wonderful with Indian dahl and saffron rice or with any vegetable curry! Try using different kinds of lentils. —Brenda

Yield: 10 3-inch croquettes

Per croquette: Cal. 177   Fat 6.5g   Sat. fat 1.0g   Sod. 169.1mg   Carb. 24.2g   Diet. fiber 4.1g   Sugars 3.3g   Prot. 7.1g

Potato-Corn Tacos

In a medium-size bowl whip the potatoes, onion powder, salt, and Tofutti Sour Supreme by hand until mixture is the consistency of lumpy mashed potatoes.

In a skillet over medium-high heat, sauté the onions in the olive oil until almost clear. Add the corn and stir until it is a light golden brown. Stir the corn mixture into the mashed potatoes until well blended.

Coat a corn tortilla lightly with an olive or canola oil nonstick cooking spray. Fold the tortilla in half without breaking it and brown lightly on both sides. Remove from the skillet and fill with 1/2 cup potato-corn mixture. The filling will help shape the taco and keep it together. Repeat process with remaining tortillas. Garnish the tops of the tacos with mild salsa and fresh chives.

My mother-in-law cannot eat beans so this taco is just right for her. It also is a fast and easy dish to prepare. The tacos can be made the night before and reheated in the oven. Garnish with the salsa and chives just before serving. These tacos are great served with a fresh garden salad and a delicious cold watermelon. —Linda

4 cups hot cooked potatoes
1 teaspoon onion powder
1/2 teaspoon salt
1/2 cup Tofutti Sour Supreme
1/2 cup diced onions
1 tablespoon olive oil
1 cup frozen or fresh corn
10 corn tortillas
1/2 cup mild salsa
1/2 cup chopped fresh chives

Yield: 10 tacos

Per taco: Cal. 148 Fat 6.2g Sat. fat 2.1g Sod. 409mg Carb. 21.8g Diet. fiber 2.5g Sugars 1.5g Prot. 2.9g

Cashew Chicken Stir Fry

4 cups hot cooked brown rice

1 tablespoon olive oil

1 cup julienned celery

2 cups julienned onions

1 1/2 cups julienned carrots

2 1/2 cups Soy Add-ums

2 cups hot water

1 tablespoon McKay's Vegan Chicken Style Seasoning

Sweet & sour sauce (recipe below)

1/2 cup roasted cashews

1 head broccoli, cut into pieces, steamed & hot

SWEET & SOUR SAUCE

1 cup apple-juice concentrate

3 tablespoons Bragg Liquid Aminos

2 tablespoons fruit-sweetened blackberry jam

1/8 teaspoon ginger

1 tablespoon fruit sweetened ketchup

2 tablespoons cornstarch

2 tablespoons cold water

Cook the rice according to package directions. In a large skillet over medium heat, heat olive oil. Add the celery and onions and sauté about 10 minutes. Add the carrots.

Heat the Soy Add-ums in hot water in the microwave for 1 to 2 minutes until soft. Drain and add to the ingredients in the skillet. Sprinkle in the Chicken Style Seasoning. Add the sweet and sour sauce to the ingredients in the skillet, stir, and remove from heat.

Roast the cashews in the microwave for 2 to 3 minutes and set aside. Put the hot brown rice on a platter and pour the stir fry on top of it leaving a little rice showing around the edge of the platter. Garnish with roasted cashews on top and fresh, steamed broccoli around the edge of the rice on the platter.

For sweet & sour sauce: In a sauce pan heat the apple-juice concentrate, Liquid Aminos, jam, ginger, and ketchup until sauce comes to a boil. Combine the cornstarch and water and stir into the sauce. Keep stirring until sauce is thickened.

For a spicy taste add a couple of small hot red peppers to the stir fry. Serve this dish with a colorful fresh vegetable tray. Remember, the more color you have at your meals the more nutrition your family is getting. Hope you enjoy this delicious healthy dish as much as we do! —Linda

Yield: 6 1/2-cup servings stir fry; 8 1/2-cup servings rice

Serving (stir fry): Cal. 284   Fat 9g   Sat. fat 1.4g   Sod. 417.9mg   Carb. 45.8g   Diet. fiber 6.4g   Sugars 8.5g   Prot. 11.4g

Black Bean Quesadillas

Blend black beans and salsa in a blender or food processor until smooth. Spread 1 tablespoon Tofutti Better Than Cream Cheese on each two whole-wheat tortillas. Make sure it is spread evenly and covers the entire tortilla. Spread 1/2 cup bean mixture on one whole-wheat tortilla. Sprinkle 1 tablespoon of green chile peppers on top of the beans. Place the other whole-wheat tortilla spread-side down on top of the beans. Grill in a medium hot, nonstick skillet on both sides. Cut each quesadilla into 4 pieces and arrange on a large platter around a small bowl of mild salsa. Garnish with fresh parsley.

I created this recipe when cooking for kids at summer camp and they loved them! Serve these delicious quesadillas with a fresh green salad, guacamole, and Tofutti Sour Supreme. —Linda

1 cup cooked black beans

1/4 cup mild salsa

4 tablespoons Tofutti Better Than Cream Cheese

8 6-inch whole-wheat tortillas

4 tablespoons green chile peppers

Fresh parsley

Yield: 4 6-inch quesadillas

Per quesadilla: Cal. 181 Fat 4.2g Sat. fat <1g Sod. 345.8mg Carb. 30.4g Diet. fiber 6g Sugars <1g Prot. 6.8g

Tamale Pie

2 14 3/4-ounce cans cream-style corn

2 14 1/2-ounce cans tomatoes, undrained

1 8-ounce can tomato sauce

1 3.8-ounce can sliced black olives (optional)

1/4 cup canola oil

1 teaspoon salt

1/2 teaspoon cumin

3 tablespoons cornstarch

1 cup yellow cornmeal

1 cup soy milk

In a large pan, boil the corn, tomatoes, tomato sauce, olives, oil, salt, and cumin for 20 minutes, stirring often. Set aside. In a medium mixing bowl, stir together the cornstarch and cornmeal. Add the soy milk and stir until just moistened. Add to the corn and tomato mixture and stir well. Pour into a 9 x 13-inch casserole dish sprayed with a nonstick cooking spray. Bake at 325 degrees for 1 hour.

I love tamales, so when I don't have time to make them this satisfies my craving! —Cinda

Yield: 12 1/2-cup servings

Serving: Cal. 225   Fat 8.1g   Sat. fat 1g   Sod. 740.9mg   Carb. 36.9g   Diet. fiber 3.8g   Sugars 4.2 g   Prot. 4.4g

Baked Corn Casserole

Preheat oven to 375 degrees. In a large mixing bowl, combine dry ingredients. Add soy milk, Tofutti Better Than Sour Cream, and oil. Mix well for 1 to 2 minutes. Add corn and mix another minute. Spray a 3-quart baking dish with a nonstick cooking spray. Pour mixture into dish. Cover the top with aluminum foil and bake for 30 minutes. Remove aluminum foil and continue baking another 30 minutes. Top should be golden in color. Serve hot!

To give it a little zing, try adding 1 cup diced green chile peppers and 1/2 cup diced jalapeño peppers before baking.—Brenda

1 cup flour

3/4 cup cornmeal

1/2 cup Pure Florida Crystals

3/4 teaspoon salt

3 teaspoons Rumford Baking Powder

2 tablespoons cornstarch

1 cup soy milk

1 8-ounce tub Tofutti Better Than Sour Cream

2 tablespoons canola oil

1 15 1/4-ounce can corn or 1 1/2 cups fresh or frozen corn

3 14 3/4-ounce cans cream-style corn

Yield: 16 1/2-cup servings

Serving: Cal. 236   Fat 6.2g   Sat. fat 2.9g   Sod. 130.1mg   Carb. 43.7g   Diet. fiber 3.1g   Sugars 10.3g   Prot. 4.9g

One-Dish Meals

Sweet Potato
Chili
p. 62

Cowboy
Tamale Pie
p. 61

Old Fashioned Chicken
& Biscuits
p. 49

Mexican Layer Casserole
p. 45

Walnut Chicken Stir-fry
p. 54

German Potato Casserole

8 cups diced cooked
potatoes

1 cup sliced vegan
hot dogs

1/2 cup Tofutti Better
Than Sour
Cream

1/2 cup sauerkraut

White sauce
(recipe below)

1 cup soy cheese

3 sprigs parsley

Grape tomatoes

WHITE SAUCE

3 cups soy milk

1 teaspoon salt

1 teaspoon seasoned
salt

1/4 cup cornstarch

1/4 cup cold water

In a large bowl, mix together the potatoes, veggie hot dogs, Tofutti Better Than Sour Cream, and sauerkraut. Set aside. Make white sauce and pour into the potato mixture. Stir until well blended. Pour potato mixture into a 2-quart baking dish and top with grated soy cheese. Bake at 350 degrees until hot and bubbly. Garnish with fresh parsley and grape tomatoes.

For white sauce: In a medium-size pan, heat the soy milk, salt, and seasoned salt. Bring to a boil. Mix the cornstarch with the 1/4 cup cold water and while stirring constantly pour into the hot, seasoned soy milk. Remove from heat as soon as the sauce is thickened.

One of my favorite vegan hot dogs is the Vibrant Life Vege-Franks. They have a wonderful taste and texture. (For more information, see Resources, p. 138.) My husband and I glean potatoes every year with our friends Darrel and Sharon Nottelson. We have lots of fun dreaming up ways we can serve this versatile food. This potato casserole is fast and easy. Serve with a colorful fresh green salad, homemade dinner rolls, and strawberry shortcake. Enjoy! —Linda

Yield: 16 1/2-cup servings

Serving: Cal. 159 Fat 4.8g Sat. fat 1.7g Sod. 201.3mg Carb. 21.9g Diet. fiber 2.5g Sugars 1.2g Prot. 7.6g

Hamburg Potato Casserole

Combine the onion and olive oil in a small microwaveable bowl with a lid. Microwave on high for 3 or 4 minutes until onions are tender. Set aside.

Brown the vegetarian burger in a large nonstick skillet. In a large bowl, mix together the potatoes, tomato soup, and onion powder. Pour potato mixture into a 3-quart baking dish coated with nonstick cooking spray. Cover the top of the tomato mixture with the burger. Sprinkle the burger with the cooked onions. Bake at 350 degrees for 25 to 30 minutes until hot and bubbly. Garnish the center with parsley and three thin slices of fresh tomato.

This casserole is one my husband's childhood favorites. So when I want to see him smile I just make him Hamburg Potato Casserole. My mother-in-law lives with us and it makes her happy to have some of her special dishes served. It brings great delight to my soul just doing the simple things that make others happy. I prefer to use Vibrant Life Vege-Burger in this recipe. (For more about Vibrant Life products, see p. 139.) *Serve with a colorful green salad, whole-wheat bread, and carob mousse cake. —Linda*

1 medium onion, diced

1 teaspoon olive oil

3 cups vegetarian burger

6 cups diced cooked potatoes

1 1/2 cups undiluted low-sodium tomato soup

1 teaspoon onion powder

3 slices fresh tomatoes

1 sprig parsley

Yield: 18 1/2-cup servings

Serving: Cal. 92   Fat 1.7g   Sat. fat <1g   Sod. 123.2mg   Carb. 11.6g   Diet. fiber 1.5g   Sugars 1.3g   Prot. 6g

Veggie Scallop Casserole

1 1/2 cups sliced onions

1 tablespoon soy margarine

4 cups soy milk

1 teaspoon onion powder

2 tablespoons McKay's Vegan Chicken Style Seasoning

1/4 cup cornstarch

1/4 cup cold water

1/2 cup Tofutti Sour Supreme

8 1/2 cups herb-seasoned breadcrumbs or cubes

3 cups frozen mixed vegetables

3 cups thinly sliced Vibrant Life Vege-Scallops or gluten

Combine the onion and margarine in a small microwaveable bowl with a lid. Microwave on high for 3 or 4 minutes until onions are tender. Set aside. In a medium-size pan combine the soy milk, onion powder, and Chicken Style Seasoning. In a small measuring cup, mix the cornstarch and cold water and set aside. Bring the seasoned soy milk to a boil and stir in the cornstarch. It will only thicken slightly as this is a thin sauce. Remove from heat and whip in the Tofutti Sour Supreme. Pour one cup of the sauce in the bottom of a 4-quart baking dish. Add 1/2 of the seasoned breadcrumbs. Next, layer the vegetables and then scallops. Top with the remaining breadcrumbs. Pour the sauce over the casserole. Sprinkle the onions and their juice on top of the sauce. Bake at 350 degrees for 40 to 45 minutes. The casserole will be a light golden brown when it is done.

This dish freezes well. Just put it together without baking it, and freeze. Take it out the night before you plan to use it so it will be thawed when you bake it. Add a little extra nonsweet soy milk to the top of the casserole if it is too dry. Then follow the baking instructions above. Garnish with fresh green onions or parsley. Serve with a colorful fresh garden salad, baked potatoes, hot dinner rolls, blackberry jam, and Brenda's Carob Peanut Butter Pie (Cooking With the Micheff Sisters, page 93). —Linda

Yield: 25 1/2-cup servings

Serving: Cal. 242   Fat 4.7g   Sat. fat 1.7g   Sod. 1034mg   Carb. 38g   Diet. fiber 4g   Sugars 2.9g   Prot. 11.7g

Mexican Layer Casserole

Combine the onion and margarine in a small microwaveable bowl with a lid. Microwave on high for 3 or 4 minutes until onions are tender. Set aside. Stir the seasoned salt into the vegetarian burger. Heat olive oil in a skillet. Add the burger and fry until slightly crispy. Set aside. Mix the tomatoes and salsa together with the onion powder. Spread 1/2 cup of the tomato mixture in the bottom of a 3-quart baking dish and place 6 of the corn tortillas on top. Spread the brown rice on top of the tortillas. Layer the chili beans over the rice. Layer the vegetarian burger on top of the beans. Cover with the 6 remaining tortillas and pour the remaining tomato mixture on top. Sprinkle the onions, the liquid from the onions, and the green chiles on top. Bake at 350 degrees for 30 to 40 minutes until hot and bubbly.

My husband loves anything that is Mexican. He doesn't even miss the cheese! But if the cheese is missed, add a cup of soy cheese to the layers and save a little to garnish the top. Serve with Tofutti Sour Supreme, oven baked tortilla chips, mild salsa, and a colorful fresh green salad. —Linda

1 cup diced onions

1 teaspoon soy margarine

2 cups Vibrant Life Vege-Burger or other vegetarian burger

1 teaspoon seasoned salt

1 tablespoon olive oil

1 1/4 cups canned diced tomatoes

1 cup mild salsa

1 teaspoon onion powder

12 6-inch corn tortillas

4 cups cooked brown rice

2 cups canned chili beans

1/4 cup green chiles

Yield: 28 1/2-cup servings

Serving: Cal. 98 Fat 1.2g Sat. fat <1g Sod. 303.7mg Carb. 16.4g Diet. fiber 2.2g Sugars 1g Prot. 4.9g

Chicken Tortilla Casserole

4 cups Soy Add-ums

3 cups water

2 tablespoons McKay's Vegan Chicken Style Seasoning

1 medium onion, thinly sliced

1 tablespoon olive oil

1 cup Tofutti Sour Supreme

1/8 teaspoon garlic powder

1 teaspoon onion powder

3 cups chili beans with sauce

18 6-inch corn tortillas

1 cup mild salsa

1/2 cup sliced black olives

In a microwaveable bowl with a lid, combine the Soy Add-ums, water, and Chicken Style Seasoning. Microwave for 2 to 3 minutes until Soy Add-ums are soft. Set aside. In a large nonstick skillet over medium heat, fry the onions in olive oil until slightly tender. Add the Soy Add-ums and fry until onions are done and Soy Add-ums are golden brown. Remove from heat and stir in the Tofutti Sour Supreme, garlic powder, and onion powder. Set aside. In a food processor, blend chili beans and their sauce until smooth. Spray a large rectangular baking dish with nonstick cooking spray and place 6 tortillas on the bottom. Spread with 1/2 of the mashed beans. Put 1/3 of the Soy Add-ums mixture on top. Layer 6 more corn tortillas on top and repeat the layers. The third layer will not have beans. Instead, pour the salsa on top of the last 6 tortillas and put the remaining Soy Add-ums mixture on top of the salsa. Bake in the oven at 350 degrees for 25 to 30 minutes or until hot and bubbly. Garnish with sliced black olives and serve.

This dish is fast and easy to put together and makes a delicious festive supper. Serve with Spanish rice, black olive salad, tortilla chips, mild salsa, and Tofutti Better Than Sour Cream. For a festive touch, use a Mexican blanket for a tablecloth and a variety of brightly colored napkins. A big sombrero filled with tortilla chips makes a great centerpiece. I find when I do special things for my family it sets the tone for a happy and fun-filled meal.
—Linda

Yield: 24 1/2-cup servings

Serving: Cal. 98   Fat 3.8g   Sat. fat 1.9g   Sod. 554.1mg   Carb. 12.5g   Diet. fiber 3g   Sugars 1.1g   Prot. 5.6g

Shepherd's Pie

In a medium saucepan, cover potatoes with water. Bring to a boil, cover, reduce heat, and simmer until tender, about 12 minutes. Drain. Add the seasoned salt and Chicken Style Seasoning to the soy milk and stir until well mixed. Pour into the potatoes and whip together with an electric mixer until potatoes are creamy. In a large mixing bowl combine the vegetarian burger and breadcrumbs. In a blender, combine the onion, tofu, Liquid Aminos, Beef Style Seasoning and onion powder. Blend until smooth and add to burger and breadcrumbs. Stir until well mixed and set aside. In a 3-quart baking dish pat the burger mixture on the bottom and sides of a bowl like a pie crust and flute the edges. Put 1/2 of the creamy potatoes on the bottom. Sprinkle the frozen peas on next. Top with the carrots. Spoon the rest of the potatoes on top. Bake at 350 degrees for 45 to 60 minutes. Cut into 28 squares and serve with brown gravy.

For brown gravy: In a 4-quart sauce pan, mix together the water, Beef Style Seasoning, salt, and Liquid Aminos. In a blender add the onion and some of the seasoned water and blend until onion is pureed. Add onion mix to the seasoned water in the sauce pan. In a medium skillet over medium heat, brown flour and set aside to cool. Sift out the lumps. In a separate bowl, mix the flour with canola oil and approximately 2 cups of the seasoned water to make a thin paste. Whip the paste into seasoned water and heat on medium-high heat, stirring until thick.

My husband loves potatoes, so this dish rates high on his list of favorites I serve it with a colorful green salad with lots of veggies, hot dinner rolls, and fruit sweetened blackberry jam. Top off the meal with homemade blueberry pie and watch your family's eyes light up with delight! —Linda

BROWN GRAVY

- 8 cups cool water
- 2 tablespoons McKay's Vegan Beef Style Seasoning
- 1/2 teaspoon salt
- 1/2 cup Bragg Liquid Aminos or soy sauce
- 1 small onion
- 1 1/2 cups unbleached white flour
- 1/2 cup canola oil

(Main ingredients)

- 8 cups russet potatoes, peeled & cut into 1 1/2-inch cubes
- 2 teaspoons seasoned salt
- 1 tablespoon McKay's Vegan Chicken Style Seasoning
- 2 cups soy milk
- 2 1/2 cups Vibrant Life Vege-Burger
- 2 cups breadcrumbs
- 1 medium onion
- 1 12.3-ounce package Mori-Nu Silken Tofu
- 2 tablespoons Bragg Liquid Aminos
- 1 tablespoon McKay's Vegan Beef Style Seasoning
- 2 teaspoons onion powder
- 1 cup frozen peas
- 4 cups crinkle-sliced carrots
- Brown gravy (recipe at left)

Yield: 28 1/2-cup servings pie; 16 1/2-cup servings gravy

Serving (pie): Cal. 120 Fat 1.1g Sat. fat <1g Sod. 165.2mg Carb. 19.5g Diet. fiber 2.3g Sugars 2.4g Prot. 6.7g
Serving (gravy): Cal. 110 Fat 6.9g Sat. fat <1g Sod. 308.6mg Carb. 10.4g Diet. fiber <1g Sugars <1g Prot. 2.1g

Mashed Potato Pie

6 medium potatoes, peeled & cut into 1 1/2-inch cubes

Salt to taste

1/2 cup soy milk

2 tablespoons soy margarine (optional)

1 cup diced onion

1 cup diced celery

1/2 cup diced red bell pepper

1 cup thinly sliced carrots

2 cloves garlic, minced

2 cups tomato sauce

1/2 cup vegetable stock

2 tablespoon vegetarian Worcestershire sauce

1 teaspoon cumin

1 teaspoon dried basil

1 teaspoon parsley

2 cups Yves Ground Round or other vegetarian burger

1 cup fresh green beans cut into bite-size pieces

1 cup corn

In a medium saucepan, cover potatoes with water and add salt if desired. Bring to a boil, cover, reduce heat, and simmer until tender, about 12 minutes. Drain and mash potatoes, adding enough soy milk for a smooth consistency. Add soy margarine if desired. Preheat oven to 375 degrees. In a skillet over medium heat, sauté the onion until clear. Add celery, pepper, carrots, and garlic. Cook until tender, 5 to 10 minutes. Stir in remaining ingredients. Bring to a boil and then simmer for five minutes. Turn off heat, cover and let stand for 15 minutes. Pour vegetable mixture into casserole dish. Spoon mashed potatoes over top, covering mixture as evenly as possible. Decorate top of potatoes using a fork to make crisscross designs. Bake for 30 minutes until top is golden. Serve hot.

You can use any vegetarian burger in this recipe but the Yves Ground Round is my favorite because it has a texture that most resembles hamburger. It also does not have a strong flavor so it takes on any flavor you give it! You can make this dish up a day or two ahead of time and keep it covered in the refrigerator. Bake 45 minutes if dish has been refrigerated. —Brenda

Yield: 20 1/2-cup servings

Serving: Cal. 108   Fat 1.5g   Sat. fat <1g   Sod. 127.9mg   Carb. 16.3g   Diet. fiber 2.6g   Sugars 1.7g   Prot. 5.7g

Old-Fashioned Chicken & Biscuits

VEGGIE STYLE

In a medium-hot skillet, sauté the onion in olive oil until clear. Add the celery and carrots and sauté 3 to 5 minutes. Add all remaining ingredients except the cold soy milk and cornstarch. Let simmer until all vegetables are tender. In a measuring cup, mix together the soy milk and cornstarch until smooth. Stir into cooked vegetables and let simmer five minutes until thickened. Serve with homemade biscuits hot from the oven! (See my niece Catie's recipe below.)

For no-shortening biscuits: Preheat oven to 425. Stir the dry ingredients together in a large mixing bowl. Pour in the oil and cut it in with a pastry blender or use two butter knives until mixture is "pebbly" in texture. Gradually stir in soy milk. Continue adding soy milk until the mixture forms a ball, separating from the sides of the bowl. Roll the dough out on a floured surface and cut into biscuits. Bake for about 10 minutes in a 425 degree oven until golden brown on the outside and slightly doughy on the inside. Serve warm. —Catie Sanner

You can also put mixture into a casserole dish and place unbaked biscuits on top. Then bake at 400 degrees for approximately 15 minutes or until biscuits are golden. Another option is to top the dish with your favorite pie crust recipe and bake at 350 degrees for 1 hour or until crust is golden. You can make this recipe a day or two prior to serving. Do not add the biscuits or pie crust until ready to put in the oven. —Brenda

1 medium onion, finely diced
1 tablespoon olive oil
1 cup diced celery
1 cup diced carrots
1 cup potatoes, peeled & diced
2 cups frozen mixed vegetables
6 cups water
6 vegetarian chicken bouillion cubes
1 tablespoon McKay's Vegan Chicken Style Seasoning
1 tablespoon parsley
1 cup Soy Add-ums or any gluten product
1 cup cold soy milk
1/3 cup cornstarch
No-shortening biscuits (recipe below)

NO-SHORTENING BISCUITS

2 cups white wheat flour (see Resources)
1 tablespoon Rumford baking powder
1/2 teaspoon salt
1/4 cup canola oil or can light olive oil
3/4 to 1 cup soy milk

Yield: 16 1/2-cup servings chicken; 10 biscuits

Serving (chicken): Cal. 67   Fat 1.8g   Sat. fat <1g   Sod. 260mg   Carb. 10.6g   Diet. fiber 2.1g   Sugars <1g   Prot. 3.1g
Per biscuit: Cal. 150   Fat 6.1g   Sat. fat <1g   Sod. 272.6mg   Carb. 20.3g   Diet. fiber <1g   Sugars <1g   Prot. 3.3g

Moroccan Vegetable Couscous

2 tablespoons soy margarine

2 tablespoons olive oil

2 medium onions, cut into small slivers

3 pinches saffron threads

1/4 teaspoon cayenne pepper

1 teaspoon turmeric

3/4 teaspoon cinnamon

1 1/2 teaspoon ginger

2 tablespoons parsley

1 teaspoon curry powder

2 cups quartered grape tomatoes

4 cups vegetable stock

3 cups water

1 medium butternut squash, peeled & cubed

1 medium turnip, peeled & cubed

4 medium zucchinis, washed & cubed

6 carrots, peeled & cut into 1/2-inch slices

6 small yellow squash, washed & cubed

1 15-ounce can chickpeas, drained & rinsed

1 1/2 cups raisins

2 tablespoons sugar

Salt to taste

4 cups uncooked quick-cooking couscous

1 cup slivered almonds, toasted

In a large saucepan over medium heat, heat margarine and olive oil. Add onions and sauté until onions are clear. Add all the spices and continue to cook for 5 minutes, stirring often. Add tomatoes, stock, and water. Bring to a boil, and then add the fresh vegetables. Cook over medium heat until vegetables are tender but firm. Add the chickpeas, raisins, sugar, and salt if using. Let simmer on low heat for another 10 minutes. Cook couscous according to package directions. Mound couscous on a large platter, and make a well in the center. Transfer vegetables to the well and sprinkle with the toasted almonds. Serve immediately.

If you have never tried couscous then this dish is a very good reason to! I have visited several Moroccan restaurants in various parts of the world and am fascinated by the unique way they flavor their dishes. Couscous is granular semolina that is served at almost every meal. It is quite different than rice and mild in taste, which makes it great for the many different foods that they put with it. I think you will enjoy the fresh vegetables mixed with the exotic flavors in this typical Moroccan dish. —Cinda

Yield: 20 1/2-cup servings

Serving: Cal. 312   Fat 7.3g   Sat. fat <1g   Sod. 732.2mg   Carb. 54.4g   Diet. fiber 6.6g   Sugars 12.4g   Prot. 9.8g

Chickpea Dahl

Cook potatoes in salted water until tender yet firm. Drain and set aside. In a medium saucepan over medium heat, sauté the onion in oil until clear. Transfer to a blender or food processor along with the tomatoes and fresh ginger and blend until smooth. Set aside. In a large saucepan, melt margarine. Add the curry powder and cumin and sauté for 4 to 5 minutes over medium heat. Stir often to avoid burning. Add the tomato mixture and continue to cook for 5 to 6 minutes, stirring often. Add the chickpeas, potatoes, frozen peas, and salt if you are using. Cook 5 to 10 minutes more. Serve hot over brown or white basmati rice.

When I began dating my husband, Joel, he introduced me to my first taste of Indian food. I love all the unusual seasonings and ingredients, and enjoy trying to create dishes from the many Indian restaurants we have eaten at. I think you will enjoy this one too! —Cinda

5 small potatoes, peeled & cut into 1 1/2-inch cubes

1 tablespoon olive or canola oil

1 1/2 cups finely chopped onion

2 cups diced canned tomatoes

2 cups sliced grape tomatoes

1 2-inch piece fresh ginger, peeled

1 tablespoon margarine

2 tablespoons curry powder

1 1/2 teaspoons cumin

2 15-ounce cans chickpeas, drained & rinsed

2 cups petite frozen peas

Salt to taste

8 cups cooked brown or white basmati rice

Yield: 16 1/2-cup servings

Serving: Cal. 175   Fat 3.3g   Sat. fat <1g   Sod. 42.2mg   Carb. 30.6g   Diet. fiber 7.2g   Sugars 4.6g   Prot. 7.4g

Spinach-Potato Curry

4 cups potatoes, sliced 1/2-inch thick

1 tablespoon canola oil

1/2 teaspoon salt

1 cup finely diced onion

2 garlic cloves, minced

2 tablespoons curry powder

1 tablespoon whole mustard seeds

1 tablespoon cumin

3 cups tomato sauce

2 cups frozen chopped spinach, thawed & squeezed dry

2 16-ounce cans garbanzo beans

1 cup vegetable broth

Drizzle potatoes with canola oil and sprinkle with salt. Place in glass 9 x 13-inch baking dish and cover with aluminum foil. Bake in 375 degree oven for about 45 minutes until potatoes are tender. Remove from oven.

In a nonstick skillet, cook the onion, garlic, curry powder, mustard seeds, and cumin for 3 to 4 minutes until onions are clear. Stir in the tomato sauce, spinach, and 1 cup of the garbanzo beans. Let simmer for 5 minutes.

In a blender combine vegetable broth and 1 cup of the garbanzo beans and process until smooth. Stir into skillet containing spinach mixture. Pour mixture over cooked potatoes and return to oven. Bake for an additional 15 to 20 minutes until mixture is hot and bubbly. Serve hot.

This is good served with pita bread and a salad! To enhance the flavor of your pita bread, heat in a skillet with just a little soy margarine, (about 1 teaspoon) turning on each side till evenly heated. Keep warm in a covered dish in the oven till ready to serve. You'll be surprised how much they will resemble the taste of the Indian bread known as "Nan." —Brenda

Yield: 16 1/2-cup servings

Serving: Cal. 116   Fat 2.5g   Sat. fat <1g   Sod. 299.9mg   Carb. 17.9g   Diet. fiber 5g   Sugars 2.7g   Prot. 5.6g

New Orleans Vegetarian Jambalaya

In a large pan over medium heat, add oil and sauté the onion, celery, red pepper, garlic, and mushrooms until vegetables are tender and onion is clear. Stir in the remaining ingredients and pour into a 3-quart baking dish sprayed with a nonstick cooking spray. Cover and bake at 350 degrees for 60 to 75 minutes until rice is tender and all liquid is absorbed.

My husband and I enjoy traveling and trying new foods. While we were in New Orleans we had some unusual and delicious dishes. I came home newly inspired and immediately began trying to recreate the ones that I had enjoyed most. This was one of my favorites! —Cinda

2 tablespoons canola or olive oil

1 large onion, finely chopped

1 cup finely chopped celery

1 red bell pepper, chopped

1 teaspoon minced garlic

2 cups sliced fresh mushrooms

3 cups diced tomatoes

2 cups water

2 tablespoons Bragg Liquid Aminos

1 cup uncooked long-grain basmati brown rice

1 tablespoon dried parsley

2 teaspoons salt

1/2 teaspoon paprika

1/4 to 1/2 teaspoon cayenne pepper

1/4 to 1/2 teaspoon chili pepper

Yield: 12 1/2-cup servings

Serving: Cal. 9 Fat 2.9g Sat. fat <1g Sod. 400.5mg Carb. 16.9g Diet. fiber 1.9g Sugars 2.9g Prot. 2.7g

Walnut Chicken Stir-fry

2 teaspoons canola oil

1 cup julienned onion

1 cup chopped red or yellow bell pepper

4 cups broccoli florets

1 1/2 cups + 1/2 cup water

1 tablespoon Bragg Liquid Aminos

2 cubes vegetarian chicken bouillon

1 teaspoon ground ginger

1 teaspoon chili powder

2 cups Soy Add-ums or gluten product of your choice

2 tablespoons cornstarch

1/2 cup walnut halves, toasted

In a large nonstick skillet or wok, sauté the onion and pepper in oil until tender.

Add broccoli and continue cooking until almost tender. Add 1 1/2 cups water, Liquid Aminos, bouillon, ginger, chili powder, and Soy Add-ums and simmer about 15 minutes. Mix together the 1/2 cup water and cornstarch and add to above dish stirring until sauce is smooth and thick. Add walnuts and serve over hot rice!

This dish is wonderful over hot brown rice or jasmine rice. If you really want to shake it up a bit, serve it over angel hair pasta! I like the nice texture that the Soy Add-ums give it but I have also used this with my homemade gluten and I like that too! —Brenda

Yield: 12 1/2-cup servings

Serving: Cal. 82   Fat 4.2g   Sat. fat <1g   Sod. 68.7mg   Carb. 8.8g   Diet. fiber 2.6g   Sugars 1.7g   Prot. 4.8g

Eggplant Roll-ups

Preheat oven to 400 degrees. In a 4-quart saucepan, add 3 quarts of water and bring to a boil. Meanwhile slice eggplant in 1/4-inch thick slices lengthwise. Discard each outside slice. (Each eggplant should yield at least seven slices.) Place slices in boiling water for 1 minute and remove. In large mixing bowl, combine tofu, onion, 1/4 cup of breadcrumbs, and 1/4 teaspoon salt. Add spinach and stir. Set aside. Sprinkle one side of each eggplant slice with the remaining seasoned breadcrumbs. Spoon tofu mixture over the crumbs and roll up eggplant slice. Place in baking dish with seam side down. Continue until all eggplant has been rolled. Cover with aluminum foil and bake at 400 degrees for 25 minutes or until eggplant is tender. Remove foil and bake for another 10 minutes. In a saucepan, combine tomatoes, tomato sauce, tomato paste, and 1/4 teaspoon salt. Stir over medium heat until it comes to a slow simmer. Spoon sauce over baked eggplant and serve hot!

I like to serve this recipe when I have company coming because it always makes my guests feel like I have fixed something special! Yet the dish is fast, fun, and easy to make! I sometimes change the filling by using herb and chive flavored Tofutti Better Than Cream Cheese instead of the tofu. It is also good with mushrooms. —Brenda

2 1-pound eggplants

1 12.3-ounce package Mori-Nu Silken Firm Tofu

1 onion, minced

1/4 cup + 3/4 cup seasoned breadcrumbs

1/4 teaspoon + 1/4 teaspoon salt

2 10-ounce packages frozen diced spinach, thawed & squeezed dry or 4 cups chopped fresh spinach

2 cups diced canned tomatoes

2 cups tomato sauce

1 8-ounce can tomato paste

Yield: 14 roll-ups

Per roll-up: Cal. 104   Fat 1.7g   Sat. fat <1g   Sod. 366.8mg   Carb. 17.3g   Diet. fiber 4.9g   Sugars 5.9g   Prot. 6.1g

Italian Goulash

1 cup sliced onions

1 tablespoon olive oil

1 cup vegetarian burger

4 cups Italian-style frozen vegetables

3 cups garlic-herb spaghetti sauce

1 teaspoon garlic powder

6 cups cooked small macaroni shells (approx. 3 cups uncooked)

In a large skillet over medium heat, sauté the onions in the olive oil. When they are almost tender, add the vegetarian burger. Any brand will do, dry or canned. (I use Worthington's canned low-fat vegetarian burger.) Add the frozen vegetables and the spaghetti sauce. Stir in the garlic powder. Simmer for 10 to 15 minutes until vegetables are tender. In a 3-quart baking dish, add the macaroni shells. Pour the vegetables and sauce on top leaving a little of the edge of the macaroni showing. Do not stir in. Garnish top with some fresh parsley. Serve immediately while it is hot.

This is a fast and easy recipe to make when you are having guests for dinner. Sometimes I make this Italian goulash the night before and then bake it the next day at 350 degrees for 15 to 20 minutes until it is hot and bubbly. I add a fresh green salad, homemade garlic bread, and blueberry pie. The blueberry pie and garlic bread can be made ahead and frozen, then taken out of the freezer a few hours before serving. The blueberry pie can either be baked first and frozen or it can be frozen unbaked. If it is frozen unbaked, allow time for it to thaw and 45 to 50 minutes baking time. The smell of the blueberry pie baking makes your guests feel right at home. This menu makes for a fast, no fuss company dinner! Set your table the night before and you will have time to relax and enjoy your guests! —Linda

Yield: 25 1/2-cup servings

Serving: Cal. 90 Fat 1.1g Sat. fat <1g Sod. 171.4mg Carb. 15.4g Diet. fiber 1.4g Sugars 1.8g Prot. 4.1g

Texas Urban Burrito

In a large saucepan over medium heat, add soy milk, flour, and salt. Stir until thickened. Add the spices and 1 cup Tofutti Better Than Sour Cream. Mix well. Add the spinach, frozen corn (you do not need to cook or thaw before adding), black beans, and chiles. Mix gently, but thoroughly. Simmer filling on low for 5 minutes. On individual plates, place one cup rice. Place filled burrito on top of the rice. Garnish with the salsa, a dollop of Tofutti Better Than Sour Cream, and soy cheese. Serve immediately.

When I make these burritos for my family, I add diced jalapeño peppers. They all like the extra spice and flavor the jalapeños give. You don't want to add too much—a little spice goes a long way! —Cinda

3 cups soy milk

3/4 cup Wondra flour

1 teaspoon salt

1 teaspoon chili powder

1 1/2 teaspoons cumin

1 tablespoon McKay's Chicken Style Seasoning

1 1/2 teaspoons Vege-Sal or other vegetable seasoning

1 teaspoon garlic powder

1 cup + 1 cup Tofutti Better Than Sour Cream or other soy sour cream

6 cups chopped fresh baby spinach

3 cups frozen sweet corn

2 15-ounce cans black beans, drained & rinsed

1 4.5-ounce can diced green chiles

12 burrito-size flour tortillas, warmed

12 cups cooked basmati brown rice, kept warm

2 cups salsa

1 cup soy cheese

Yield: 12 servings

Serving: Cal. 718 Fat 18.6g Sat. fat 8.7g Sod. 1186mg Carb. 115.2g Diet. fiber 13.6g Sugars 5.2g Prot. 25.2g

Southwestern Chili Spaghetti

1 tablespoon canola or olive oil

1 cup minced onion

1 cup diced red bell pepper

1 clove garlic, minced

3 cups water

4 cups diced canned tomatoes

1/2 cup diced green chiles

2 teaspoons minced jalapeño peppers

1/2 cup taco sauce

3 teaspoons chili powder

Salt to taste

1/4 teaspoon ground cinnamon

4 ounces uncooked spaghetti, broken in thirds (approx. 1 1/2 cups)

2 cups drained, rinsed black beans

2 cups drained, rinsed pinto beans

1 cup Tofutti Better Than Sour Cream

In a 4-quart saucepan, heat oil over medium heat. Add onion, red pepper, and garlic. Sauté 3 to 5 minutes until tender. Stir in water, tomatoes, chiles, jalapeños, taco sauce, and seasonings. Bring to a boil, reduce heat, and simmer uncovered for 5 minutes, stirring occasionally. Stir in spaghetti and return to boil. Boil gently for 10 minutes until pasta is tender. Stir in beans and continue cooking until hot and bubbly. Garnish with Tofutti Better Than Sour Cream and additional jalapeños if desired.

For something special pour this chili spaghetti in a glass casserole dish, mix up Grandma's Corn Bread (recipe on p. 137), pour the batter on top, and bake about 30 minutes at 350 degrees until corn bread is done. You can test it by inserting a toothpick. When the toothpick comes out clean, it is done! All you need now is a crisp green salad and your meal is complete! —Brenda

Yield: 23 1/2-cup servings

Serving: Cal. 111   Fat 3.1g   Sat. fat 2g   Sod. 226.9mg   Carb. 17.3g   Diet. fiber 3.8g   Sugars 3.8g   Prot. 4.4g

Baked Nachos Supreme

In a large bowl, mix together tomato sauce and salsa. Pour 1/2 the tomato sauce mixture into a 13 x 9-inch glass baking dish. Place 4 cups tortilla chips on bottom and sides of dish. Pour chili beans on top of chips. Add 1/2 cup black olives. Cover with remaining sauce and layer with 4 cups tortilla chips, olives, and beans. Crush remaining tortilla chips. Sprinkle top of casserole with crushed chips and jalapeño peppers. Cover with aluminum foil and bake at 350 degrees for 30 minutes. Remove aluminum foil and continue baking for an additional 10 to 15 minutes until chips are golden.

You can top this dish with soy cheese if desired. I like to add shredded lettuce and fresh diced tomatoes right before serving! Serve with taco sauce and you have a complete meal. You don't have to wait for company to serve this yummy dish. —Brenda

2 cups tomato sauce

2 cups mild salsa

1 cup sliced black olives

4 cups chili beans, mild or hot

8 cups + 1 cup tortilla chips

1 tablespoon minced jalapeño peppers

Yield: 20 1/2-cup servings

Serving: Cal. 223 Fat 11g Sat. fat 2g Sod. 786.2mg Carb. 32.5g Diet. fiber 4.8g Sugars <1g Prot. 5.4g

Mexicali Skillet Dinner

3 cups uncooked elbow macaroni

1 medium onion, diced

1 tablespoon olive oil

1 package Yves Ground Round or 2 cups vegetarian burger

1 4.5-ounce can diced green chiles

2 14.5-ounce cans stewed tomatoes, Mexican-style

1 15-ounce can pinto beans, drained, but not rinsed

2 tablespoons vegetarian Worcestershire sauce

1/2 cup grapeseed oil Vegenaise

1 cup crushed tortilla chips

Cook macaroni in salted boiling water until tender, set aside. In a large saucepan, sauté onions in the olive oil until clear. Add the vegetarian burger and continue cooking until burger browns slightly. Add the chiles, tomatoes, beans, Worcestershire sauce, and Vegenaise. Stir well. Stir in the macaroni. Serve in bowls with crushed tortilla chips on top.

You can also put the mixture into a casserole dish, sprinkle with the crumbled tortilla chips, and heat in the oven until bubbly. This is a quick and easy dish my whole family loves. Sometimes I add some soy cheese to it. Of course, my husband always adds hot sauce to his! —Cinda

Yield: 16 1/2-cup servings

Serving: Cal. 230   Fat 9.5g   Sat. fat 1g   Sod. 240.5mg   Carb. 27.4g   Diet. fiber 3.3g   Sugars 2.8g   Prot. 8.3g

Cowboy Tamale Pie

In a large saucepan, sauté the onion in the 1 cup of water until the onion is clear. Add the carrots, garlic, and red bell pepper and continue to cook over medium heat for 5 minutes. Add the remaining ingredients and mix well. Let simmer over low heat for 5 to 10 minutes. Spray a 9 x 13-inch baking dish with a nonstick cooking spray and pour the mixture into the dish. Cover with your favorite corn bread recipe and bake according to the corn bread directions until the corn bread is golden brown and baked through. Serve hot.

I can just picture a group of tired cowboys sitting around the evening fire eating large servings of this out of old tin plates! Sometimes just for fun I put a red kerchief tablecloth on the table and serve this to my family out of old tin pie pans. Some field or wild flowers in a canning jar make a great centerpiece. I serve individual ice cold lemonades in smaller canning jars. Add fruit cobbler for dessert and your family just might start their own ranch! —Cinda

1 medium onion, diced

1 cup + 1/2 cup water

3 large carrots, peeled & cut into large pieces

1 teaspoon minced fresh garlic

1 medium red bell pepper, chopped

1 tablespoon McKay's Vegan Chicken Style Seasoning

3 cups diced tomatoes (grape tomatoes if available)

1 7-ounce can diced green chiles

2 teaspoons ground cumin

1 16-ounce can dark red kidney beans, drained, but not rinsed

1 16-ounce can Great Northern beans, drained & rinsed

1 16-ounce can pinto beans, drained & rinsed

1 6-ounce can tomato paste

1 tablespoon oregano

Salt to taste

Your favorite corn bread recipe

Yield: 16 1/2-cup servings

Serving: Cal. 118 Fat <1g Sat. fat <1g Sod. 369mg Carb. 22.9g Diet. fiber 6.3g Sugars 4.6g Prot. 6.6g

Sweet Potato Chili

1 medium onion, minced

1 cup water

4 large carrots, peeled & cut into small chunks

1 large red bell pepper, chopped

1 teaspoon minced garlic

6 cups sweet potatoes, peeled & cut into bite-size chunks

2 cups roasted peanuts

1 28-ounce can crushed tomatoes in juice

1 6-ounce can tomato paste

2 4.5-ounce cans diced green chiles

3 tablespoons chili powder, or more if you like spicy food

1 tablespoon ground cumin

1 tablespoon sugar

1 to 2 teaspoons curry powder, to taste

Salt to taste

10 cups cooked brown rice, kept warm

In a large saucepan, sauté the onion in 1 cup of water until clear. Add the carrots, red bell pepper, and garlic and continue to cook for 5 to 6 minutes. Add the remaining ingredients and bring to a boil. Reduce heat to low and simmer gently, stirring occasionally, for 15 to 25 minutes, until the sweet potatoes are tender. If the chili is too thick, you may add a little more water during cooking. Adjust the seasonings to your liking. Serve hot over brown rice.

This is a different and delicious twist from the old familiar standby. The exotic flavors combined with the various textures of the vegetables remind me of Middle Eastern foods. —Cinda

Yield: 20 1/2-cup servings

Serving: Cal. 267   Fat 8.7g   Sat. fat 1.3g   Sod. 185mg   Carb. 42.3g   Diet. fiber 6.2g   Sugars 7.5g   Prot. 7.9g

Meat Substitutes

Salisbury Veggie-Steaks
with Brown Gravy
p. 68

Bistro Loaf
p. 82

Vegetarian
Fish Sticks
p. 85

Pecan Oatmeal
Patties
p. 81

Apricot
Walnut Balls
p. 78

Mushroom Steaks

1 20-ounce can Worthington Vegetable Steaks, reserve broth

1 cup seasoned flour (recipe below)

Mushroom gravy (recipe at right)

SEASONED FLOUR

1 cup white wheat flour (see Substitutions on p. 11)

1/2 cup nutritional yeast

1 tablespoon McKay's Vegan Beef Style Seasoning

1 tablespoon McKay's Vegan Chicken Style Seasoning

1 tablespoon Vege-Sal

1/2 teaspoon onion powder

1/4 teaspoon garlic powder

MUSHROOM GRAVY

3 tablespoons cornstarch

3 tablespoons cold water

1/2 cup minced onions

1 tablespoon soy margarine

3 cups soy milk

1/2 cup broth from Vegetable Steaks

1/2 teaspoon salt

1/4 teaspoon seasoned salt

1/2 cup Tofutti Better Than Sour Cream

1/2 cup finely chopped canned mushrooms

Slice the Vegetable Steaks into thin pieces. Dip both sides of Vegetable Steaks into the seasoned flour. Place on a greased baking tray and bake at 350 degrees for about 20 to 25 minutes or until browned on one side. Place in a 2-quart baking dish and pour mushroom gravy over the top of the steaks. Bake until hot and bubbly.

For seasoned flour: In a mixing bowl combine all ingredients.

For mushroom gravy: In a small cup, mix the cornstarch and cold water and set aside. Combine the chopped onion and soy margarine in a small microwaveable bowl with a lid. Microwave on high for 3 or 4 minutes until onions are tender. Set aside. In a medium saucepan, combine the soy milk, broth, salt, and seasoned salt. Bring to a simmer over medium heat. Add the cornstarch mixture. Stir over heat until soy milk is thickened. Remove from heat. Add the Tofutti Better Than Sour Cream and stir until well blended. Add mushrooms and onions. Stir until well blended. Pour over Vegetable Steaks and bake at 350 degrees for 15 to 20 minutes or until hot and bubbly.

You can also make this entree with 3 cups of homemade gluten pieces instead of the Vegetable Steaks. I like to serve these steaks with mashed potatoes, green beans, cooked carrots, a vegetable tray, homemade dinner rolls, and strawberry shortcake. This gravy recipe will also make a great noodle casserole if you add cooked pasta noodles before baking. And, you can turn this mushroom gravy into celery soup! That's right, my friend Lesa Budd gave me the idea. Just omit the mushrooms and stir in 1/2 teaspoon of celery salt and 1/2 cup cooked chopped celery. Add soy milk until it reaches a cream-soup consistency, and enjoy! —Linda

Yield: 6 1/2 servings steaks; 8 1/2-cup servings gravy

Serving (steaks): Cal. 197 Fat 1.6g Sat. fat <1g Sod. 1180mg Carb. 26.8g Diet. fiber 6.5g Sugars 0.3g Prot. 18.8g
Serving (gravy): Cal. 107 Fat 5.8g Sat. fat 3g Sod. 246.5mg Carb. 10.4g Diet. fiber <1g Sugars 1.6g Prot. 3.5g

Fake Steaks

In a blender, combine walnuts, oats, yeast flakes, onion powder, garlic powder, and warm water. Process 1 to 2 minutes until smooth. Pour into bowl of a heavy-duty mixer. Using the "dough hook," mix in gluten flour and process 3 to 4 minutes until dough is smooth and forms into a rubberlike ball. Remove dough and divide into two parts. Form each part into a log shape about 2 inches around. Slice each log into 1/4-inch slices. Drop slices into boiling broth. When all slices are in the broth, simmer slowly 1 to 2 hours. Steak pieces will almost double in size and color of steaks will lighten. Remove from broth and use in any recipe asking for gluten steaks or grind and use in place of hamburger.

For broth: Combine all ingredients into a large stockpot. Bring to a boil and let simmer 15 minutes prior to adding steaks.

I like to use these steaks for many different recipes. I place the steaks on a baking sheet, sprayed with nonstick cooking spray, and bake at 350 for 30 minutes. This changes the texture to a slightly more "chewy" consistency. Then I place the steaks in a baking dish and pour mushroom soup over them and bake at 350 for 1 hour. Delicious and easy! I also like these steaks in sandwiches. Try frying the steaks with onions. Place in baking dish, pour canned tomatoes on top, and bake for one hour. You'll love it! This is a favorite Sabbath dish in our home. Put it in the oven before church, set the oven to precook and you'll walk in the house after church to wonderful smells! —Brenda

1 cup walnuts

1 1/4 cups rolled oats

1/2 cup nutritional yeast flakes

1 teaspoon onion powder

1 teaspoon garlic powder

1 3/4 cups warm water

2 1/2 cups gluten flour

Broth (recipe below)

BROTH

12 cups water

1 cup Bragg Liquid Aminos or soy sauce

1 medium onion, diced

1 teaspoon salt (optional)

Yield: 40 2-inch steaks or 2 quarts steaks

Per steak: Cal. 53   Fat 2.2g   Sat. fat <1g   Sod. 4.4mg   Carb. 4.2g   Diet. fiber 1g   Sugars <1g   Prot. 5.6g

Salisbury Veggie-Steaks

1 cup diced onions

2 tablespoons olive oil

3 cups ground gluten

3 cups cracker crumbs

1 12.3-ounce package Mori-Nu Silken Firm Tofu

1 teaspoon onion powder

1 tablespoon McKay's Vegan Chicken Style Seasoning

1 tablespoon McKay's Vegan Beef Style Seasoning

1/4 teaspoon garlic powder

1/2 teaspoon rosemary

4 cups brown gravy (recipe on p. 47)

Combine the onion and olive oil in a small microwaveable bowl with a lid. Microwave on high for 3 or 4 minutes until onions are tender. Set aside. In a large mixing bowl, add gluten and onions. In the blender, blend tofu and seasonings until smooth. Pour into the gluten mixture. Mix well. Form into oval shapes 1/2-inch thick and 3 1/2 inches long. Spray a nonstick baking sheet with nonstick cooking spray and place the oval steaks on the tray. Bake at 350 degrees for 15 minutes. Turn over and bake another 15 minutes. The Veggie-Steaks will be a golden brown color when they are done. Serve with brown gravy.

My mother-in-law loves these Veggie-Steaks. I know when she likes something it must be good! She is a wonderful cook and always makes such tasty foods. These steaks can be baked and cooled and then frozen. They will keep a couple of months in the freezer. I love to have entrees like this on hand for my drop-in guests. I even keep my table set just in case someone stops by unexpectedly. I always keep in mind the Bible text that reminds us "some have entertained angels unawares" (Hebrews 13:2). —Linda

Yield: 15 3 1/2-inch steaks

Per steak: Cal. 177   Fat 7.3g   Sat. fat 1.3g   Sod. 375.8mg   Carb. 13.8g   Diet. fiber 2.8g   Sugars 1.1g   Prot. 14.8g

Veggie-Steaks & Tomatoes

Drain steaks and reserve the liquid. Slice each steak in half. Mix the flour and nutritional yeast flakes together in a large plastic bag. Add the vegetable steak slices and shake until well coated. Spray a large baking sheet with a nonstick cooking spray. Put the coated steak slices in a single layer on the baking sheet. Bake in a 375 degree oven for about 30 minutes, turning over after 15 minutes, until veggie steaks are browned and slightly crispy. Meanwhile, in a medium saucepan over medium heat, sauté the onions in oil until clear. Set aside. Put the steaks into a large casserole dish that has been sprayed with a nonstick cooking spray. Pour the reserved liquid from the cans over the top. Scatter the sautéed onion over the steaks. Pour the tomatoes over the onions. Stir slightly and bake in a 375 degree oven for 45 minutes to 1 hour until steaks are browned and crispy. Serve hot.

2 20-ounce cans Worthington Low-Fat Vegetable Steaks (or any gluten steaks)

2 cups flour

1 cup nutritional yeast flakes

1 medium onion, slivered

1 tablespoon canola oil

2 16-ounce cans crushed tomatoes

This is one of my all-time favorite dishes. My mom used to make this for Sabbath dinner when I was little and we all loved it. Now whenever my kids come home from school they almost always ask me to make this! You can use homemade gluten if you cannot find the Worthington Vegetable Steaks. You can also make this without the onions if you prefer. —Cinda

Yield: 16 1/2-cup servings

Serving: Cal. 176   Fat 2.4g   Sat. fat <1g   Sod. 90.8mg   Carb. 24.1g   Diet. fiber 7.9g   Sugars <1g   Prot. 17.2g

Veggie-Chicken Roll

1 frozen Vibrant Life Chicken Roll, thawed

3 tablespoons canola or olive oil

1 large onion, chopped

2 cups finely chopped celery

2 tablespoons McKay's Vegan Chicken Style Seasoning

1 cup quick oats

1 cup seasoned breadcrumbs

1 12.3-ounce package Mori-Nu Silken Tofu

1 cup chopped pecans

1/2 cup Toffutti Better Than Sour Cream

1/2 cup vegetable broth

1 package puff pastry

Chicken-style gravy (recipe below)

CHICKEN-STYLE GRAVY

3 1/2 cups water

3/4 cup Wondra flour

3 tablespoons McKay's Vegan Chicken Style Seasoning

1 to 2 tablespoons margarine

1 tablespoon parsley flakes

Carve a hole in the middle of the chicken roll all the way to the end of the roll. Hollow out the middle leaving an inch all the way around the roll. Grate the chicken pieces that have been hollowed out of the middle of the chicken roll. Set aside. Sauté onion and celery in oil until onion is clear and celery is tender and place in large mixing bowl. Add the remaining ingredients except puff pastry and gravy. Mix well.

Fill the middle of the chicken roll with the dressing mixture. Spray a nonstick cookie sheet or pan with vegetable spray and place the chicken roll on the tray. Place the rest of the dressing firmly around the sides and on top of the chicken roll, covering completely. Take both sheets of puff pastry long ways and press the ends together, making a tight seal. Cover entire chicken roll with the puff pastry. Cut off the excess of dough leaving one inch all around the dough. Tuck the puff pastry under the chicken roll. Take the extra dough and with a mini leaf cutter cut out leaves and garnish the top of the puff pastry with the leaves. Bake at 350 degrees for 45 minutes or until the top is golden and crispy. Serve with chicken-style gravy.

You can also prepare this recipe as a loaf: Grate 2 1/2 cups Vibrant Life Chicken Roll. Prepare dressing as directed above. Pour into a medium casserole dish sprayed with a nonstick cooking spray. Bake in a 350 degree oven for 45 minutes until top is golden and crispy. Slice into squares and serve with the chicken-style gravy.

For chicken-style gravy: Mix water, flour, and Chicken Style Seasoning together in a medium saucepan. Heat over medium heat, stirring constantly until thickened. Add the margarine and parsley and mix well. Serve hot.

The only vegan chicken roll I have found is the Vibrant Life brand. I make this for holidays and special occasions. Serve this elegant chicken roll and dressing on a bright colored platter with vegetables and roasted red potatoes as shown on the cover of our cook book. This is not only a delicious entrée but it makes a beautiful center piece as well.

Yield: 32 servings

Serving: Cal. 293   Fat 17g   Sat. fat 3g   Sod. 912mg   Carb. 19g   Diet. fiber 1.5g   Sugars 1.3g   Prot. 17g

Tofu Turkey Loaf

In microwave or in a skillet, cook onions, garlic, and celery in water until tender. Pour into large mixing bowl. Add remaining ingredients. Mix well. Add additional water if mixture is too dry. Do not get the mixture too wet; it should be just moist enough to hold together well. Pour into a medium baking dish and bake for one hour at 375 degrees until top is golden and crispy. Serve hot!

You don't have to wait till Thanksgiving to enjoy this. My husband loves this anytime. You can substitute the Special K *cereal with corn flakes or a similar cereal. I have also used soda crackers. This just helps "bind" it together thus omitting the need for eggs. You can also make this dish a day or two ahead of time and bake it before serving. I don't recommend freezing as this will change the texture. You will want some leftovers, though, because this is also good sliced and served cold in sandwiches! —Brenda*

1 medium onion, minced

2 cloves fresh garlic, minced

1/2 cup finely chopped celery

1/2 cup water

1 14-ounce package water-packed tofu

1 cup shredded carrots

2 cups chopped fresh mushrooms

2 cups *Special K* cereal

2 cups stuffing mix

1 teaspoon sage

1/2 teaspoon basil

1 teaspoon thyme

1 teaspoon powdered mustard

2 tablespoons McKay's Vegan Chicken Style Seasoning

Yield: 12 1/2-cup servings

Serving: Cal. 85   Fat 1.4g   Sat. fat <1g   Sod. 448.6mg   Carb. 13.5g   Diet fiber 1.1g   Sugars 2.8g   Prot. 4.9g

Mock Chicken Loaf

2 cups Soy Add-ums

3 tablespoons McKay's Vegan Chicken Style Seasoning

1/2 teaspoon sage

4 cups hot water

7 1/2 cups seasoned croutons

2/3 cup pecans, toasted

1/4 cup olive oil

2 cups sliced green onions

1 cup chopped celery

1 tablespoon soy margarine

In a large bowl, mix the Soy Add-ums, Chicken Style Seasoning, sage, and hot water. Let sit at least five minutes. Add the croutons, pecans, and olive oil. Put the green onions, celery, and the soy margarine in a glass bowl with a lid. Cover and microwave 4 to 5 minutes until onions are soft in texture. Add the onions and celery to mix in the bowl. Mix together and pour into a large baking dish that has been sprayed with a nonstick vegetable spray. Bake at 350 degrees for 40 to 45 minutes. Serve with your favorite cranberry sauce.

My husband loves this dish served with mashed potatoes and gravy. To make the meal complete I add a green vegetable, corn on the cob, homemade dinner rolls with blueberry jam, and a colorful fresh garden salad. I love making my husband feel like he is "important company," so I top the meal off with a frozen strawberry smoothie garnished with pecans and fresh blueberries . . . umm . . . umm . . . good! —Linda

Yield: 20 1/2-cup servings

Serving: Cal. 179 Fat 12.7g Sat. fat 1.8g Sod. 447.5mg Carb. 13.5g Diet. fiber 2.5g Sugars 2.7g Prot. 4.3g

Marrakech Roast

Add the bulgur wheat, sage, oregano, and salt if you are using it, to 2 cups water in a saucepan. Bring to a boil. Slow boil until tender and chewy. Blend 1/2 the garbanzos with the remaining 1 cup water. In a medium skillet, sauté the onions, pepper, and celery until the onions are clear and the celery and pepper are tender. Mix all ingredients together and pour into a medium casserole dish that has been sprayed with a nonstick cooking spray. Bake at 350 degrees for 1 hour. The top will get crunchy and brown. You can cover the top with foil for the last 15 minutes of baking if you do not like the top to be crunchy.

I gave this recipe a Middle Eastern name because bulgur wheat is a staple grain of Middle Eastern diets. Bulgur is whole wheat that has been steamed, dried, and then cracked. It is not to be confused with cracked wheat, which is uncooked. I sometimes will bake this mixture in tomatoes or red bell peppers that have been hollowed out. It is delicious and is especially nice when serving buffet-style. —Cinda

2 cups bulgur wheat
1/2 teaspoon sage
1/2 teaspoon oregano
Salt to taste
2 cups + 1 cup water
2 16-ounce cans garbanzo beans, drained & rinsed
1 small onion, finely chopped
1 medium red bell pepper, finely chopped
1 cup finely chopped celery
2 tablespoons olive oil
1/2 cup sliced black olives
1/2 cup finely chopped tomatoes

Yield: 20 1/2-cup servings

Serving: Cal. 114 Fat 2.9g Sat. fat <1g Sod. 35.2mg Carb. 18.7g Diet. fiber 4.4g Sugars 2.2g Prot. 4.6g

Cashew Roast

3 tablespoons canola or olive oil

1 large onion, finely chopped

3 stalks celery, finely chopped

3 cups finely ground toasted cashews

2 cups vegetarian burger

1 cup soy milk

2 tablespoons cornstarch

1 tablespoon McKay's Vegan Beef Style Seasoning

1 tablespoon Bragg Liquid Aminos

1/2 teaspoon salt

1/2 cup grapeseed Vegenaise

In a medium skillet, heat the oil. Sauté onions and celery until onion is clear and celery is tender. Put in a large mixing bowl. Add remaining ingredients and mix well. Spray a medium casserole dish with a nonstick cooking spray. Pour mixture into the dish and cover with foil. Set the casserole in a shallow pan of water. Bake at 350 degrees for 45 minutes. Uncover and remove from water. Bake 15 more minutes. Cut into squares and serve hot with ketchup or gravy.

I love the flavor that the roasted cashews give this roast. You can toast the cashews in a skillet on medium heat or in the microwave. Either way, be SURE to stir often as the nuts can burn very fast. They will deepen in color and become very fragrant when ready. —Cinda

Yield: 20 1/2-cup servings

Serving: Cal. 196   Fat 13.7g   Sat. fat 2.4g   Sod. 218mg   Carb. 10.8g   Diet. fiber 1.3g   Sugars 1.7g   Prot. 7.7g

Farmer's Roast

In a medium skillet over medium heat, sauté onion and mushrooms in the oil until onion is clear. In a large bowl, mix together the remaining ingredients except gravy. Spray a medium casserole dish with a nonstick cooking spray and add roast mixture. Place in the casserole dish. Bake at 350 degrees for 1 hour. Serve with country gravy.

For country gravy: In a medium skillet, brown flour, stirring constantly with a wire whisk until it becomes fragrant and slightly deeper in color. Add the yeast flakes and oil and cook, stirring for just a minute more. Add the water all at once, whisking fast and continuously until thickened. This will only take a minute or so. Add the Liquid Aminos or soy sauce and salt to taste. Serve hot.

You can make this roast into patties and either fry in a skillet or brown in the oven. You can also serve it with many different types of gravies, which makes it a very versatile entree. I serve it with a big bowl of mashed potatoes, corn on the cob, and tomatoes and cucumbers fresh from my husband's garden. If you can't live on a farm, this is the next best thing! —Cinda

COUNTRY GRAVY

1/2 cup whole-wheat flour

1/2 cup nutritional yeast flakes

1/3 cup oil

2 1/2 cups cool water (may add more to obtain desired consistency)

4 tablespoons Bragg Liquid Aminos or soy sauce

Salt to taste

---

1 medium onion, finely chopped

1 1/2 cups finely chopped fresh mushrooms

3 tablespoons canola or olive oil

2 cups vegetarian burger

2 cups cooked brown rice (recipe on p. 17)

1/2 cup quick oats

2 cups seasoned breadcrumbs

1/2 cup grapeseed Vegenaise

1 teaspoon Vege-Sal or other seasoned vegetable salt

1 tablespoon dried parsley

1 cup chopped walnuts

1/2 cup soy milk

Country gravy (recipe at left)

Yield: 20 1/2-cup servings roast; 12 1/4-cup servings gravy

Serving (roast): Cal. 181   Fat 8.5g   Sat. fat 1g   Sod. 259.1mg   Carb. 17.3g   Diet. fiber 2.1g   Sugars 1.2g   Prot. 8g
Serving (gravy): Cal. 96   Fat 6.2g   Sat. fat <1g   Sod. 6.541mg   Carb. 7.5g   Diet. fiber 3.6g   Sugars <1g   Prot. 4.7g

Portobello Pecan Loaf

2 cups chopped
  portobello
  mushrooms

1 medium onion,
  finely minced

1 teaspoon onion
  powder

1 medium onion

1 12.3-ounce package
  Mori-Nu Silken
  Firm Tofu

1 cup seasoned
  breadcrumbs

4 cups quick oats

2 cups crushed saltine
  crackers

2 cups chopped pecans

1/2 teaspoon salt

1 teaspoon garlic
  powder

1 teaspoon onion
  powder

1 teaspoon sage

1/2 teaspoon thyme

1/2 teaspoon oregano

1/2 teaspoon cayenne
  pepper

1 cup cooked lentils

1 cup cooked brown rice

Soy milk (as needed
  to moisten)

2 cans low-sodium
  tomato soup

2 cups water

In a medium skillet over medium heat, sauté mushrooms, onions, and onion powder together until tender. Set aside.

Puree whole onion and tofu in food processor until smooth. Pour mixture into a large mixing bowl. Add breadcrumbs, oats, crackers, pecans, seasonings, lentils, and brown rice. Mix well. Add soy milk a little at a time until mixture sticks together.

Spray a medium baking dish with nonstick cooking spray. Place 2/3 of the mixture into the baking dish. Mold into a loaf shape. Push down mixture in center, making an indentation about 1 1/2 inches deep in middle. Leave 2-inch "walls" on each side of the loaf. Fill indentation with mushroom mix. Cover filling with the remaining loaf mixture, carefully sealing the edges. Mix tomato soup and water and pour over loaf and down the sides. Bake at 350 degrees for 1 1/2 hours. Serve hot.

It is always a treat when your guests discover the hidden Portobello surprise inside. I like to put baked potatoes and butternut squash in the oven so the meal is complete and ready all at the same time! Add a green salad and you're all set! —Brenda

Yield: 20 1/2-cup servings

Serving: Cal. 238 Fat 10.1g Sat. fat 1.1g Sod. 235.4mg Carb. 30.7g Diet. fiber 4.5g Sugars 3.6g Prot. 8g

Special K Roast

Sauté onion in olive oil or margarine until it is clear. Combine remaining ingredients and mix well. Spray a medium casserole dish with a nonstick cooking spray. Pour mixture into the casserole dish. Bake at 350 degrees for 40 to 45 minutes. Top should be brown and slightly crispy. Cut into squares and serve hot.

This is a healthier version of an old family favorite. I like to serve this with ketchup, but it is also good with brown gravy. You can freeze it before baking but let it thaw completely before you bake it. My husband likes to make sandwiches with the leftovers! —Cinda

1 medium onion, minced

1/4 cup olive oil or margarine

1 cup finely chopped pecans

1 cup finely chopped walnuts

2 12.3-ounce packages Mori-Nu Silken Firm or Extra-Firm Tofu

1 tablespoon McKay's Vegan Chicken Style Seasoning

1 teaspoon Vege-Sal or other vegetable seasoning

1/4 cup nutritional yeast flakes

1 12-ounce box or 7 cups *Special K* cereal

1 1/2 cups soy milk

Yield: 12 1/2-cup servings

Serving: Cal. 293   Fat 19.3g   Sat. fat 2.1 g   Sod. 319.1mg   Carb. 20.2g   Diet. fiber 3g   Sugars 4g   Prot. 12.7g

Apricot Walnut Balls

4 tablespoons water

1 medium onion

2 tablespoons finely minced fresh parsley

2 teaspoons McKay's Vegan Chicken Style Seasoning

2 cloves garlic, finely minced

1 1/2 cups finely crushed saltine crackers

1 cup finely chopped walnuts

1 cup oats

1 12-ounce package extra-firm tofu

Apricot sauce (recipe below)

APRICOT SAUCE

1 1/2 cups apricot jam

1 cup fruit-sweetened ketchup

1/2 cup lemon juice

4 tablespoons evaporated cane juice crystals

4 tablespoons finely minced onion

1 tablespoon canola oil

1 teaspoon salt

1/2 teaspoon dried oregano

In food processor, puree the water and onion until smooth. Pour into large mixing bowl. Add remaining ingredients except apricot sauce. Mix until mixture holds together.

Coat hands with nonstick cooking spray. Shape mixture into 1-inch balls. Place balls on a baking sheet and bake for 30 minutes at 375 degrees. Remove from oven and place in a medium baking dish. Pour apricot sauce over the meatballs and bake an additional 30 minutes. Serve hot!

These walnut balls can be made ahead of time and frozen. Pour the sauce on them when you are ready to bake and serve. I have also used them with other sauces—even for spaghetti and meatballs! Try making the balls a little smaller for an appetizer! For a crispier texture, instead of baking them, fry them in a little canola oil until crispy and golden. They are good this way without the sauce! —Brenda

For apricot sauce: In a small saucepan, combine all ingredients. Bring to a boil. Pour over baked (or fried) walnut balls and return to oven for an additional 30 minutes.

For something different you can fry the walnut balls and then use this recipe for a dipping sauce. This is especially good when using this dish as an appetizer. —Brenda

Yield: 32 1-inch walnut balls

Per walnut ball: Cal. 73 Fat 3g Sat. fat <1g Sod. 119.9mg Carb. 11g Diet. fiber <1 g Sugars 9g Prot. 1.3g

Garbanzo Pecan Balls

In a blender, add the tofu, onion, water, Beef Style Seasoning, and Liquid Aminos. Blend until creamy. In a large mixing bowl, combine the breadcrumbs and pecan meal. Add the tofu mixture. Put the garbanzos into the blender and blend until the beans are in fine pieces and add to the rest of ingredients. Mix until well blended. Form into small balls. (I used a size 50 scoop.) Place on a greased cookie sheet and bake for 40 to 45 minutes at 350 degrees.

These veggie meatballs are delicious in a marinara sauce and served over pasta. They can also be baked in the oven with low-sodium tomato or mushroom soup until bubbly and hot. I like to serve them with baked potatoes, fresh broccoli, corn on the cob, fresh green salad, homemade bread, and blueberry pie. Make a double batch and place in your freezer for those special times when you need to make a meal in a hurry! You don't even need to thaw them before baking! —Linda

- 1 12.3-ounce Mori-Nu Silken Tofu
- 1 medium onion
- 1/4 cup cold water
- 1 tablespoon McKay's Vegan Beef Style Seasoning
- 2 tablespoons Bragg Liquid Aminos
- 4 cups seasoned breadcrumbs
- 1 cup pecan meal
- 1 1/2 cups cooked or canned garbanzos

Yield: 50 1-inch "meatballs"

Per "meatball": Cal. 54 Fat 4.2g Sat. fat <1 g Sod. 208.9mg Carb. 9.2g Diet. fiber 1.3g Sugars 1g Prot. 2.8g

Breaded Tofu Patties

2 cups cooked potatoes

1 12.3-ounce package Mori-Nu Silken Tofu

1/4 cup grapeseed oil Vegenaise

1 8-ounce container Tofutti Herb & Chives Better Than Cream Cheese

2 teaspoons all-purpose salt-free seasoning

1 tablespoon McKay's Vegan Chicken Style Seasoning

2 cups quick oats

1 cup finely chopped onions

1 tablespoon soy margarine

1 cup cooked garbanzos

1 cup herb-seasoned breadcrumbs

Mash the potatoes and tofu together in a large bowl. Add the Vegenaise, Better Than Cream Cheese, seasonings, and the quick oats to the potatoes and tofu and mix together. Put the onions and margarine in a glass bowl with a lid and microwave for 3 to 4 minutes or until onions are tender. Add the onions to the rest of the ingredients. In a blender or food processor blend the garbanzos with 1/4 cup cold water and add to the rest of the ingredients. Stir until well mixed. Place the breadcrumbs in a bowl. Measure 1/4 cup of the tofu mixture, pat it gently into a round thick patty. Press it into the breadcrumbs, breading on both sides. Spray a cookie sheet with nonstick vegetable spray and place patties on sheet. Bake at 350 degrees for 20 minutes, turn over and bake 20 additional minutes until golden on both sides. Serve with your favorite gravy, fruit-sweetened ketchup, or just as they are.

I like to serve these tofu patties with fresh broccoli, sweet potatoes, garden fresh salad, homemade bread, and Roxanna Jam Cookies (Cooking With the Micheff Sisters, p. 101) for dessert. For good digestion start your meal with praises to God. Psalm 144:15 reminds us: "Happy are the people whose God is the Lord." Now enjoy your meal! —Linda

Yield: 25 patties

Per patty: Cal. 144   Fat 7.2g   Sat. fat 1.1g   Sod. 354.7mg   Carb. 15g   Diet. fiber 1.8g   Sugars 1.1g   Prot. 5.1g

Pecan Oatmeal Patties

Preheat oven to 375 degrees. Spray baking sheet with nonstick cooking spray.

In a large mixing bowl, combine oatmeal, onion, 4 tablespoons spaghetti sauce, pecans, yeast flakes, seasonings, active dry yeast, and 1/2 cup breadcrumbs. Mix well. Mixture should be just wet enough to hold together and shape into patties. Add additional spaghetti sauce if mixture is too dry. If you get it too wet, don't panic—just add additional breadcrumbs and it should be just fine!

Mix together 2 cups breadcrumbs with cayenne pepper, if using. Form patty mixture into 3-inch patties. Press patties gently into pepper-crumb mixture and turn over, coating both sides evenly.

Place on baking sheet that has been sprayed with a nonstick cooking spray. Spray nonstick cooking spray on top of patties as well. Bake in oven at 375 degrees for 30 minutes. Remove from oven and turn patties over. Spray tops again with the nonstick cooking spray. Return to oven and continue baking for an additional 30 minutes or until patties are golden and crisp. Serve hot!

I like to serve these with a baked potato, fresh vegetable, and a salad. I have to hide the platter though as they tend to disappear before I can get the rest of the food on the table! If you don't like spicy food, just omit the cayenne pepper in the crumb mixture. This is a good dish to make when you have leftover oatmeal from breakfast! —Brenda

2 cups cooked oatmeal, cooled & firm

1 medium onion, minced

4 tablespoons + more as needed spicy spaghetti sauce

1/2 cup chopped pecans

1 tablespoon nutritional yeast flakes

1 teaspoon garlic powder

1/2 teaspoon dried basil

1 teaspoon onion powder

1/2 teaspoon ground coriander

1/2 teaspoon salt

1/2 teaspoon sage

1/2 teaspoon active dry yeast

1/2 cup + 2 cups seasoned breadcrumbs

1/2 teaspoon cayenne pepper (optional)

Yield: 15 3-inch patties

Per patty: Cal. 132   Fat 4.3g   Sat. fat <1g   Sod. 479.8mg   Carb. 19.6g   Diet. fiber 2.5g   Sugars 1.7g   Prot. 4.4g

Bistro Loaf or Patties

1 cup brown basmati rice

1 cup diced sweet potato

1 cup chopped carrots

1 cup bulgur wheat

1 1/4 cups boiling water

1 medium onion chopped

1 tablespoon canola oil

1 cup quick oats

1/2 12.3-ounce package Mori-Nu Silken Firm Tofu

1/2 cup breadcrumbs

1/4 cup coarse Dijon mustard

1 cup chopped pecans

6 tablespoons pecan meal

1/4 cup Bragg Liquid Aminos

2 tablespoons onion powder

2 tablespoons garlic powder

2 tablespoons chili garlic hot sauce

1 cup ketchup

1/4 cup water

Cook the rice according to package directions. Cool. Roast sweet potato and carrots in glass dish at 400 degrees in oven until tender. Pour boiling water over the bulgur wheat and cover until the water is absorbed and the bulgur is tender. In a medium skillet over medium heat, heat oil and sauté onion until clear. In a large bowl, mix together rice, sweet potato, carrots, bulgur, oats, tofu, breadcrumbs, mustard, pecans, pecan meal, sautéed onion, Liquid Aminos, onion powder, garlic powder, and hot sauce.

Shape mixture into a loaf shape and place it in the middle of a medium casserole dish, leaving at least an inch between the loaf and the dish. Mix ketchup and water together and pour over loaf, covering all sides. Bake at 375 degrees for 1 hour. Serve hot.

Or: Shape mixture, a 1/2 cup at a time, into patties and place on an oiled baking sheet. Bake at 375 to 400 degrees for 30 minutes. Serve with brown gravy or mushroom gravy.

I love this recipe! It is packed with nutrition. I usually double it and it feeds a crowd! If I don't need both roasts, I freeze one for later. Sometimes I make half of the recipe into patties and freeze them for another meal. Any leftovers make great sandwiches. —Cinda

Yield: 30 1/2-cup servings loaf or patties

Serving: Cal. 122   Fat 6.1g   Sat. fat <1 g   Sod. 67.8mg   Carb. 14.7g   Diet. fiber 2.2g   Sugars 1.6g   Prot. 3.3g

Mushroom Pecan Burgers

Preheat oven to 375 degrees. Spray baking sheet with nonstick cooking spray. In a medium skillet over medium heat, sauté the onions in oil about 5 minutes until clear. Add the marjoram, thyme, and mushrooms. Cook stirring often, 5 to 10 minutes more, until the mushrooms are tender.

Spoon the mushroom mixture into a large bowl. Add remaining ingredients. Mix well until mixture holds its shape.

Shape into patties and place them on the prepared baking sheet. Bake for 25 minutes. Turn patties over and return to oven for about 25 minutes until golden brown. Serve hot.

These are also good fried in a skillet with a small amount of olive oil. I bake them in the oven to keep my fat grams to a minimum. You can freeze these patties after baking. They are not only good as a main entree but also as a burger in a sandwich. I like to keep a supply in the freezer for a quick dinner for unexpected company! —Brenda

1 cup finely minced onions

1 tablespoon olive oil

1/2 teaspoon dried marjoram

1/4 teaspoon dried thyme

2 cups chopped fresh mushrooms

2 teaspoons McKay's Vegan Chicken Style Seasoning

1 cup chopped pecans, toasted

2 teaspoons Bragg Liquid Aminos

1 cup plain breadcrumbs

1 cup cooked brown rice

1 cup rolled oats

1 16-ounce package tofu, drained & rinsed

Salt to taste

Yield: 16 3-inch burgers

Per burger: Cal. 139   Fat 7.3g   Sat. fat <1g   Sod. 129.7mg   Carb. 14.4g   Diet. fiber 2 g   Sugars 1.7g   Prot. 5.2g

Veggie-Burgers

1 12.5-ounce package
  Mori-Nu Silken
  Tofu

1 small onion

2 tablespoons Bragg
  Liquid Aminos
  or soy sauce

2 teaspoons Vege-Sal

1 19-ounce can Vibrant
  Life Vege-Burger

1 to 2 cups crushed
  saltine crackers

Fruit-sweetened
  ketchup
  (recipe below)

FRUIT-SWEETENED
KETCHUP

1 12-ounce can
  tomato paste

1/8 teaspoon garlic
  powder

1/2 teaspoon seasoned
  salt

1/2 teaspoon onion
  powder

1/2 teaspoon salt

6 ounces undiluted
  apple-juice
  concentrate

2 tablespoons fresh-
  squeezed lemon
  juice

In a blender blend the tofu, onion, Liquid Aminos, and Vege-Sal until smooth and creamy. In a mixing bowl, mix together the burger, crackers, and creamy tofu mixture. Form into 3-inch patties and fry in a nonstick pan with a little olive oil. Serve with fruit-sweetened ketchup.

I can still remember my childhood and the inviting smells coming from Mom's kitchen. I especially loved her veggie burgers with homemade buns. Now that I have a home of my own I enjoy sharing some of Mom's recipes with my family and friends. These veggie-burgers are a spin-off of my Mom's burgers. When I was a child we used eggs to make these. Now we all are searching for healthier ways to feed our families. These burgers can be made in the oven instead of fried on the stove. Spray a cookie sheet with vegetable spray and then place the veggie burgers on the tray and spray the tops of the burgers. Bake them at 350 degrees for about 20 minutes or until golden brown. The burgers can also be frozen for up to a couple of months. Keep in mind that cooking is more than making food. It's also making memories.
—Linda

For fruit-sweetened ketchup: Blend until all ingredients are well mixed. Place in a container and chill in the refrigerator.

This ketchup will keep a couple of weeks in the refrigerator. —Linda

Yield: 15 3-inch burgers; 24 tablespoons ketchup

Per burger: Cal. 80 Fat <1g Sat. fat <1g Sod. 54.2mg Carb. 7.4g Diet. fiber 1g Sugars <1g Prot. 8.5g
Per tablespoon ketchup: Cal. 27 Fat <1g Sat. fat <1g Sod. 64.6mg Carb. 6.5g Diet. fiber <1g Sugars 1.5g Prot. <1g

Vegetarian Fish Sticks

In a medium-size bowl put the Soy Add-ums and 2 cups of water and set aside for 10 to 15 minutes to soak. When the Soy Add-ums are soft, put them in a food processor along with whatever water is left and chop into fine pieces. Put the onions and margarine in a glass bowl and microwave for approximately 3 to 4 minutes until onions are tender. In a large bowl, put the Soy Add-ums, onions, breadcrumbs, Chicken Style Seasoning, onion powder, cooked oatmeal, and quick oats. Mash the tofu with a fork and then add it to the breadcrumbs.

Break the seaweed into pieces in a food processor. Add 1 tablespoon hot water and whiz until it makes a smooth paste. Mix the seaweed paste into the breadcrumbs. Stir until well mixed.

Shape the mixture, 1/4 cup at a time, into 1 x 4-inch sticks. Place the sticks on a cookie sheet that has been sprayed with a nonstick cooking spray. Spray the tops of the fish sticks and bake in the oven at 350 degrees for 40 to 45 minutes. Serve with tartar sauce.

For tartar sauce: Mix all ingredients together and refrigerate until cold. Serve with fish sticks.

These "fish sticks" are good fried in olive oil and served on a whole-wheat bun with lettuce, tomato, onions, and tarter sauce. Add a fresh fruit plate, a bowl of popcorn, and a fruit smoothie to finish off the meal. Invite some friends over for fellowship. We love to spend time with our family and friends around the table together just sharing how God has blessed in all our lives. In Psalms 34:8 it says, "Taste and see that the Lord is good," and somehow I think that God is talking not only about food for our bodies but also food for our souls! Truly, He is good! —Linda

Yield: 25 fish sticks; 16 tablespoons tartar sauce

2 cups Soy Add-ums

2 cups water

1 cup finely diced onions

1 tablespoon margarine

2 cups herb-seasoned breadcrumbs

3 tablespoons McKay's Vegan Chicken Style Seasoning

1 teaspoon onion powder

1/2 cup cooked quick oats

3 cups quick oats

1 12.3-ounce package Mori-Nu Silken Tofu

2 sheets seaweed

2 tablespoons hot water

2 teaspoons salt-free all-purpose seasoning

Tartar sauce (recipe below)

TARTAR SAUCE

1/2 cup Tofutti Better Than Sour Cream

1/4 cup grapeseed oil Vegenaise

1/4 cup chopped lemon-dill pickles

1/8 teaspoon turmeric (optional)

Per fish stick: Cal. 103 Fat 2.2g Sat. fat <1g Sod. 318.9mg Carb. 16g Diet. fiber 2.1g Sugars 1.2g Prot. 5.4g
Per tablespoon tartar sauce: Cal. 27 Fat 2.4 g Sat. fat 1.4g Sod. 61mg Carb. 0.9g Diet. fiber <1g Sugars <1g Prot. <1g

Mock Crab Cakes

1 medium onion,
    finely chopped

1 cup finely chopped
    celery

1 tablespoon olive oil

2 cups cooked
    brown rice

2 16-ounce packages
    water-packed firm
    tofu, rinsed &
    drained

2 cups whole-wheat
    breadcrumbs,
    from fresh bread

1/2 cup Vegenaise or
    soy mayonnaise
    substitute

1/4 cup chopped fresh
    or dried parsley

1 teaspoon crushed
    basil

1 teaspoon salt

1/2 cup Seafood
    Seasoning Mix
    (recipe at right)

1/3 cup crushed
    seaweed sheets

1 tablespoon powdered
    kelp

1 teaspoon lemon juice

Crumb mix
    (recipe at right)

Fresh parsley

Grape tomatoes

Tartar sauce
    (recipe at right)

SEAFOOD SEASONING MIX

1 cup nutritional yeast
    flakes

2 tablespoons onion
    powder

2 teaspoons garlic
    powder

2 teaspoons paprika

1 teaspoon celery seed

2 teaspoons turmeric

2 teaspoons dried
    parsley

2 tablespoons McKay's
    Vegan Chicken
    Style Seasoning

CRUMB MIX

2 cups seasoned
    breadcrumbs

2 tablespoons paprika

TARTAR SAUCE

1 cup Vegenaise

1/2 teaspoon salt

1/2 cup sweet relish

1 teaspoon onion
    powder

1 1/2 tablespoons
    lemon juice

3 tablespoons
    dehydrated onion

1 to 2 tablespoons
    honey

In a blender put seaweed sheets and 2 tablespoons hot water and process till smooth. Set aside. In a skillet, sauté onions and celery in olive oil until clear. Put in a large mixing bowl and add rice, tofu, breadcrumbs, Vegenaise, seasonings, seaweed mixture, kelp, and lemon juice. Mix together until mixture will just hold together to form a patty. If too dry, add a little extra Vegenaise. If too wet, add extra breadcrumbs.

Gently press crab cakes into crumb mix and place on a baking sheet sprayed with a nonstick cooking spray. Spray tops of cakes with nonstick cooking spray. Bake in a 375 degree oven for 30 minutes. Remove from oven and spray with nonstick cooking spray. Turn cakes over gently using a spatula. Spray tops of cakes with nonstick cooking spray and return to oven for an additional 30 minutes or until golden and crispy. Remove from oven and place on a serving platter. Garnish with parsley and grape tomatoes. Serve with tartar sauce.

For crumb mix: Mix breadcrumbs and paprika together in small bowl.

Yield: 24 3-inch cakes;
36 2-teaspoon servings tartar sauce

Per cake: Cal. 148 Fat <1g Sat. fat <1g Sod. 447.4mg Carb. 20.9g Diet. fiber 2.4g Sugars 1.3g Prot. 6.9g
Per serving tartar sauce: Cal. 28 Fat 1.8g Sat. fat 0g Sod. 104.5mg Carb. 2.7g Diet. fiber 0g Sugars <1g Prot. <1g

Mock Crab Cakes

For Seafood Seasoning Mix: Blend all ingredients together in a blender till smooth. Let mixture sit for 1 minute before removing blender lid. Seafood Seasoning Mix may be stored in a covered glass container in a cupboard up to 3 months.

For tartar sauce: Mix all ingredients together. Refrigerate for 1 to 2 hours until cold. Add more honey if you like it sweeter, or more lemon juice if you like it a bit more tart.

These are wonderful for anyone missing that seafood flavor! The kelp and seaweed in this recipe give it the fishy taste. I think you could almost fool someone into thinking this was the real thing! If you don't like seafood, this is not the recipe for you! —Brenda

Pasta

Penne: A Little South
of the Border!
p. 96

Bowtie Asparagus and
Sun-dried Tomato
p. 100

Rotelle
Primavera
p. 92

Capellini
Pomodoro
p. 108

Sweet Potato
Ravioli
p. 101

Rotelle Primavera

2 cups peeled & diced
eggplant

1 teaspoon salt

2 tablespoons olive oil

1 cup chopped onions

1 cup julienned
carrots

1 cup broccoli florets

1 cup cauliflower
florets

3 cups spaghetti sauce

1 teaspoon garlic
powder

2 teaspoons all-
purpose no-salt
seasoning

1 teaspoon onion
powder

1 teaspoon Italian
seasoning

4 cups cooked rotelle
pasta

1 cup cooked frozen
or fresh spinach

1/2 cup sliced
almonds, roasted

Cover eggplant with water. Stir in salt. Let eggplant sit for 4 to 5 minutes in the salted water then drain. In a medium-hot skillet, add the oil and sauté the onions, carrots, and eggplant. Stir often. When the onions are almost tender, add the broccoli, cauliflower, spaghetti sauce, and seasonings. Simmer for about 15 minutes. Mix the rotelle pasta in with the vegetables and sauce and pour into a 3-quart dish. Sprinkle the cooked spinach and almonds on top. Serve immediately.

Rotelle pasta has a short, fat screwlike shape. It is sometimes called fusilli. If you cannot get this kind just use any kind of your favorite pasta. To make this dish even better add some sliced cooked red bell peppers and zucchini. Serve this dish with garlic breadsticks, a fresh green salad full of vegetables. Top off your meal with homemade apple pie (Cooking With the Micheff Sisters, p. 121). —Linda

Yield: 20 1/2-cup servings

Serving: Cal. 126   Fat 5.2g   Sat. fat <1g   Sod. 141.4mg   Carb. 17.6g   Diet. fiber 2.8g   Sugars 1g   Prot. 3.2g

Mexican Rotini

Sort and wash the lentils. Put the lentils, water, salt, and brewers yeast flakes in a medium saucepan and cook on medium-high heat for 30 to 40 minutes until lentils are a saucelike consistency. Add the salsa, tomatoes, and seasoning to the lentils. In a medium skillet over medium heat sauté the onions in the olive oil. When the onions are clear, add them to the lentil mixture and simmer for 5 to 10 minutes. Put 3 cups corn chips in a large casserole dish. Spread 1/2 of the lentil mixture on top of the chips and then put the rotini on top of the lentils. Spread the remaining lentils on top until all the pasta is covered. Top with remaining chips, olives, and grape tomatoes. Serve with Tofutti Sour Cream and mild salsa.

If using canned red lentils just drain the juice, blend them in the blender, and then add to the salsa, diced tomatoes, onions, and seasonings and simmer for 20 to 25 minutes. I like to cook extra lentils and freeze them so that when I have drop-in company I can put a meal together with no fuss. I serve this dish with a green salad and Carob Mousse Cake. —Linda

1 cup dry red lentils

4 cups hot water

1 teaspoon salt

4 teaspoons brewers yeast flakes

1 cup mild salsa

3 1/2 cups diced tomatoes

2 teaspoons all-purpose salt-free seasoning

3/4 cup diced onions

1 tablespoon olive oil

3 cups + 1 cup oven-baked corn chips

4 cups cooked rotini

1/2 cup sliced black olives

1/2 cup sliced fresh grape tomatoes

Tofutti Sour Cream

Salsa

Yield: 28 1/2-cup servings

Serving: Cal. 86   Fat 1.4g   Sat. fat <1g   Sod. 183.8mg   Carb. 14.5g   Diet. fiber 1.7g   Sugars 1g   Prot. 4.1g

Spicy Chili Rotini

4 cups uncooked
    rotini pasta

1 medium onion,
    finely minced

1 cup chopped celery

2 cloves fresh garlic,
    finely minced

2 tablespoons olive oil

1 package Yves
    Ground Round
    Burger or 2 cups
    other vegetarian
    burger

3 cups undrained hot
    chili beans

4 cups canned diced
    tomatoes

1 teaspoon Pure
    Florida Crystals

1/2 teaspoon cayenne
    pepper

1/2 teaspoon salt

3 tablespoons chili
    powder

1 tablespoon
    vegetarian
    Worcestershire
    sauce

Cook pasta according to package directions. Drain and set aside.

In a large skillet, sauté the onion, celery, and garlic in the olive oil. Cook until the onion and celery are tender. Add the remaining ingredients. Simmer 15 to 20 minutes. Add pasta and serve.

This is very similar to a dish that our mom made when we were kids. She always put elbow macaroni pasta in it which is good too. In this recipe I made it a bit spicier and used rotini pasta which I love! You can use this recipe with any pasta, even spaghetti! You can also use any vegetarian burger that you wish. My favorite is always the Yves burger. —Brenda

Yield: 10 1/2-cup servings

Serving: Cal. 255   Fat 2.8g   Sat. fat <1g   Sod. 476.5mg   Carb. 46.3g   Diet. fiber 4.1g   Sugars 4.2g   Prot. 11.1g

Old El Paso Chili Casserole

In a large saucepan, add 1 cup water, Chicken Style Seasoning, and the onion. Cook until the onion is clear. Add the vegetarian burger and continue to cook for 3 to 4 minutes more, stirring frequently. Stir in the uncooked noodles, 2 more cups water, tomato paste, stewed tomatoes, salsa, and salt if using. Cover and let simmer on low for 15 minutes. Add the frozen corn and mix well. Pour the mixture into a large baking dish and bake at 350 degrees for 30 minutes.

This is really a fun and delicious casserole to make because, depending on the type of pasta and salsa you use—it can turn out different every time you make it! —Cinda

1 cup + 2 cups water

1 tablespoon McKay's Vegan Chicken Style Seasoning

1 medium onion, chopped

2 cups vegetarian burger

1 14-ounce box fettuccine noodles, broken into thirds

1 6-ounce can tomato paste

2 14.5-ounce cans Mexican-style stewed tomatoes, broken into small pieces

1 1/2 cups mild or medium salsa

Salt to taste

2 cups frozen corn

Yield: 28 1/2-cup servings

Serving: Cal. 95   Fat <1g   Sat. fat <1g   Sod. 216.3mg   Carb. 14.6g   Diet. fiber 1.3g   Sugars 1.2g   Prot. 6.5g

Penne: A Little South of the Border!

1 large onion, chopped

2 large red bell peppers, cut into 1/4-inch slices

2 tablespoons canola oil or olive oil

2 cups thinly sliced vegetarian sausage links

1 tablespoon finely minced garlic

3 14.5-ounce cans petite diced tomatoes

2 8-ounce cans tomato sauce

1 to 1 1/2 teaspoons crushed red pepper

1 pound penne pasta, cooked al dente

Salt to taste

In a large skillet over medium heat, heat oil and sauté the onion and bell peppers until the onion is clear. Add the vegetarian sausage and garlic and sauté 3 to 4 minutes more. Add remaining ingredients. Mix well. Pour mixture into a large baking dish and bake uncovered for 20 to 25 minutes in a 400 degree oven. Serve hot.

If you do not like spicy foods, use less of the crushed red pepper or leave it out completely. If you like, assemble this dish a day ahead, refrigerate, and bake just before serving. Sometimes I like to add black beans and frozen corn to this dish, and then sprinkle crushed corn chips on top! —Cinda

Yield: 36 1/2-cup servings

Serving: Cal. 57   Fat 1g   Sat. fat <1g   Sod. 160.4mg   Carb. 8.52g   Diet. fiber 1.3g   Sugars 2.9g   Prot. 3.3g

Wild Mushroom Penne

In a large skillet over medium heat, sauté onion and mushrooms in the margarine until the onion is clear. Add garlic and sauté another minute. Sprinkle flour over the top and mix well. Cook, stirring constantly, for 1 minute. Pour in the soy milk, apple cider, and seasonings. Mix well, and continue stirring 3 to 4 minutes until the sauce thickens. Set aside. Cook the penne pasta according to package directions until almost al dente. Drain pasta, but do not rinse. Add to the saucepan, along with the peas and parsley. Mix well and heat just until hot. Serve immediately. If the sauce is too thick, thin it with vegetable stock or soy milk.

When I was a little girl, I can remember certain times of the year when Grandpa would go on mushroom hunts. He would disappear into the woods and return with buckets of tender mushrooms. Grandma would fry them with onions and we would eat them along with hearty loaves of European-style country bread. This recipe reminds me of those days, and perhaps that is why I love this dish so much! —Cinda

1/2 cup minced onion

2 cups sliced baby portobello mushrooms

1 cup sliced shiitake mushrooms

2 tablespoons margarine

1 clove garlic, minced

2 tablespoons unbleached white flour

1 3/4 cups soy milk

1/4 cup unsweetened apple cider

2 teaspoons McKay's Vegan Beef Style Seasoning

1 1/2 teaspoons Dijon mustard

1/2 teaspoon dried tarragon

1/2 teaspoon dried oregano

1/2 teaspoon dried basil

4 cups uncooked penne pasta

1 cup frozen petite peas

1/2 cup dried parsley

Salt to taste

Yield: 10 1/2-cup servings

Serving: Cal. 160   Fat 2.4g   Sat. fat <1g   Sod. 829.8mg   Carb. 29.2g   Diet. fiber <1g   Sugars <1g   Prot. 4.7g

Creamy Vegetable Penne

4 cups soy milk

1 cup Soy Silk Creamer

1 teaspoon seasoned salt

1/2 teaspoon celery salt

1 teaspoon onion powder

1/4 teaspoon garlic powder

6 tablespoons cornstarch

6 tablespoons cold water

1 12.3-ounce package Mori-Nu Tofu

1 teaspoon salt

1 cup steamed onions

1 cup sliced & stemmed broccoli pieces

1 cup cooked julienned carrots

1 pound penne pasta, cooked

1 tablespoon minced fresh or dried parsley

In a medium saucepan heat the soy milk, Soy Silk Creamer, seasoned salt, celery salt, onion powder, and garlic powder. Mix the cornstarch and cold water together until the cornstarch is dissolved. Just before the hot soy milk comes to a boil stir in the cornstarch. Keep stirring until it thickens and then remove from the heat.

In a blender put the tofu, salt, and steamed onions. Blend until smooth. Mix into the soy milk sauce. Add the broccoli pieces and carrots.

Put the hot penne pasta in a casserole dish and pour the sauce over the pasta. Sprinkle parsley on top. Serve immediately.

This recipe can be made up the day before you need it and then baked in the oven right before serving. Bake at 350 degrees for 20 to 25 minutes until it is hot and bubbly. God made so many wonderful colorful vegetables not only for us to enjoy eating but to help us stay healthy. So serve a colorful vegetable salad with your meal, some whole-wheat dinner rolls with strawberry jam, and top your meal off with No-Bake Tofu Cheesecake topped with fresh blueberries (Cooking With the Micheff Sisters, p. 123). *And give thanks to God for He is good!* —Linda

Yield: 28 1/2-cup servings

Serving: Cal. 74 Fat 2g Sat. fat <1g Sod. 115.3mg Carb. 11.1g Diet. fiber <1g Sugars 1.9g Prot. 3.1g

Manicotti

In a blender put the tofu, Better Than Cream Cheese, garlic powder, lemon juice, onions, Chicken Style Seasoning, Italian seasoning, and water. Blend until smooth. Spray a large baking dish with vegetable spray and pour 2 cups of the spaghetti sauce in the bottom. Fill each manicotti with the tofu mixture and place on top of the spaghetti sauce. Spread remaining tofu mixture on top of the manicottis. Pour spaghetti sauce down the middle of each row of manicottis and sprinkle the garlic powder on top of the sauce. Bake at 350 degrees for 20 to 30 minutes until hot and bubbly. Sprinkle the top of the manicottis with dried parsley just before serving.

This is an especially quick and easy meal to make. Accompany the manicotti with homemade garlic bread, garden fresh salad, homemade cookies, and enjoy the bonding time with family and friends! —Linda

2 12.3-ounce packages Mori-Nu Tofu

1 8-ounce container Herb Seasoned Better Than Cream Cheese

1 1/4 teaspoons garlic powder

1/2 teaspoon lemon juice

1/2 cup minced onions

1 teaspoon McKay's Vegan Chicken Style Seasoning

1/2 teaspoon Italian seasoning

1/4 cup water

2 cups + 1 cup spaghetti sauce

14 cooked manicotti

2 tablespoons dried parsley

Yield: 14 3-inch manicottis

Serving: Cal. 168   Fat 5g   Sat. fat <1g   Sod. 474.3mg   Carb. 22.7g   Diet. fiber 1.9g   Sugars 3.9g   Prot. 7.8g

Bowtie Asparagus & Sun-dried Tomato

1 medium onion, minced

2 tablespoons soy margarine

1 cup water

4 vegetarian chicken bouillon cubes

2 cups soy milk

1/2 cup chopped sun-dried tomatoes

1/2 teaspoon onion powder

1/4 teaspoon dried marjoram

1/4 teaspoon dried basil

1/4 teaspoon dried oregano

2 teaspoons chili powder

1 teaspoon Pure Florida Crystals

4 cups diced fresh asparagus

4 cups uncooked bowtie pasta

Cook pasta according to package directions until al dente. Drain and set aside. Cut asparagus into 1 1/2-inch pieces and set aside.

While pasta is cooking, sauté onion in soy margarine in a large skillet until onion is clear. Add bouillon cubes, soy milk, tomatoes, seasonings, and brown sugar. Simmer for 15 to 20 minutes, and add asparagus pieces. Cook 1 to 2 minutes until asparagus is slightly tender and add cooked bowtie pasta. Serve hot!

Al dente is Italian for "to the tooth" and describes pasta that is not soft or overdone. I love bowtie pasta so I use it in quite a few recipes. Try adding whole black olives for added color and texture. This has a nice light sauce and is great for a buffet because it tastes great hot or cold! If serving hot, it is best to cook right before serving. —Brenda

Yield: 16 1/2-cup servings

Serving: Cal. 195 Fat 3.3g Sat. fat <1g Sod. 911.4mg Carb. 35.5g Diet. fiber 1.1g Sugars 2g Prot. 6.1g

Sweet Potato Ravioli

Mix together until smooth 2 cups sweet potatoes, salt, margarine, cinnamon, and nutmeg and set aside.

Divide pasta dough into sixths. Roll each sixth to a 9 x 9-inch square, approximately 1/16-inch thick. With a pasta cutting wheel or knife cut into 9 equal pieces, making 3-inch squares. Dip finger or a small pastry brush in water and go around edges of squares to moisten. Place 1 heaping teaspoon of filling on each center of half of the squares. Cover with the remaining squares. Push down edges until completely sealed. Press the tips of a fork around all four edges of each ravioli. Boil gently in salted water for approximately 10 minutes until tender. Drain and place in casserole dish. Drizzle with sweet potato sauce and serve hot!

I tasted something very similar at a restaurant once and loved it so much I went home and tried to recreate it. I actually like mine better because this recipe has a lot less fat and no dairy. When I am in a hurry, I have used Chinese wonton wrappers instead of my homemade pasta and it works too! —Brenda

For sweet potato sauce: Put all ingredients in blender and process until very smooth. Pour into a medium saucepan and bring to a soft boil. Turn down heat and simmer about five minutes until slightly thickened. Drizzle over raviolis and serve hot!

This sauce is so good I have actually served it for a soup! It's so easy to make, but your guests will think you cooked for hours! Sweet potatoes are a favorite of mine and one vegetable that I never get tired of! —Brenda

2 cups mashed baked sweet potatoes

1 teaspoon salt

1 tablespoon margarine

1/4 teaspoon cinnamon

1/4 teaspoon nutmeg

Homemade Eggless Pasta (recipe on p. 102)

Sweet potato sauce (recipe below)

SWEET POTATO SAUCE

2 cups mashed baked sweet potatoes

4 cups soy milk

1 tablespoon margarine

1/4 teaspoon nutmeg

1/4 teaspoon cinnamon

1/8 teaspoon onion powder

3 vegetarian chicken bouillon cubes

3 to 4 tablespoons Wondra flour

Yield: 27 3-inch ravioli; 12 1/2-cup servings sauce

Per ravioli: Cal. 36 Fat 1g Sat. fat <1g Sod. 200.2mg Carb. 6.4g Diet. fiber 1g Sugars 2.6g Prot. <1g
Per serving sauce: Cal. 84 Fat 2.6g Sat. fat <1g Sod. 137.5mg Carb. 11.8g Diet. fiber 1.2g Sugars 3.1g Prot. 3.6g

Portobello Ravioli

1 medium onion, minced

2 tablespoons margarine

4 cups chopped portobello mushrooms

Salt to taste

1/4 teaspoon marjoram

1 teaspoon basil

1 teaspoon oregano

Pinch rosemary

2 tablespoons herb & chive flavor Tofutti Better Than Cream Cheese

Homemade Eggless Pasta (recipe below)

8 cups spaghetti sauce

HOMEMADE EGGLESS PASTA

4 cups semolina flour

1 teaspoon salt

1 1/2 cups warm water

Sauté onion in margarine in a medium skillet until onion is clear and tender. Add mushrooms and seasonings. Cook until mushrooms are tender. Remove from heat and let cool. Add Tofutti Better Than Cream Cheese to cooled mixture. Mix well and set aside. Divide pasta dough into sixths. Roll each sixth to a 9 x 9-inch square, approximately 1/16-inch thick. With a pasta cutting wheel or knife cut into 9 equal pieces, making 3-inch squares. Dip finger or a small pastry brush in water and go around edges of squares to moisten. Place 1 heaping teaspoon of filling on each center of half of the squares. Cover with the remaining squares. Push down edges until completely sealed. Press the tips of a fork around all four edges of each ravioli. Boil gently in salted water for approximately 10 minutes until tender. Drain and place in a casserole dish. Heat spaghetti sauce and pour over raviolis. Serve hot!

You can substitute Chinese wonton wrappers in place of the pasta dough. You can also freeze the fresh uncooked raviolis and use as needed. My husband likes this so much that we've made it our Friday-night tradition along with fresh asparagus and vegan Caesar salad. —Brenda

For Homemade Eggless Pasta: In a large mixing bowl, mix flour and salt. Add warm water all at once and stir quickly to make stiff dough. Add additional water if needed. Form the dough into a ball and knead for 10 minutes adding an additional sprinkle of flour if dough is sticking to bowl. Cover and let dough rest for 20 to 30 minutes. Roll out dough with a rolling pin as directed above.

I have tried this with all-purpose flour, but is makes tougher pasta so I definitely recommend the semolina flour. You can find it in most natural food stores. —Brenda

Yield: 27 3-inch raviolis; 16 1/2-cup servings eggless pasta

Per ravioli: Cal. 72 Fat 2.4g Sat. fat <1g Sod. 398.8mg Carb. 10.9g Diet. fiber 2.5g Sugars 6.2g Prot. 2.5g
Per serving pasta: Cal. 114 Fat <1g Sat. fat <1g Sod. 146.4mg Carb. 23.8g Diet. fiber <1g Sugars 0g Prot. 3.2g

Garden Fettuccine

Stir the olive oil into the cooked fettuccine and set aside. In a large skillet add the water, cabbage, carrots, red peppers, and onions. Cover and cook the vegetables on medium-high heat until tender. Add the spaghetti sauce, seasonings, and salsa and simmer for about 15 minutes. Remove from heat and add the fettuccine and steamed broccoli. Stir gently until well mixed. Pour into a large bowl and top with fresh chives and parsley.

I like to serve this with a fresh vegetable salad, garlic bread, and a bowl of fresh strawberries. This is a simple and fast meal to prepare and has lots of antioxidants in it that are so good for our bodies. I love the way the apostle John expresses God's desires for us in 1 John 3: "Beloved, I pray that you may prosper in all things and be in health, just as your soul prospers." Isn't it wonderful that we can enjoy our food with God's wonderful blessings!
—Linda

1/2 pound fettuccine, cooked

1 tablespoon olive oil

1 cup water

2 cups shredded cabbage

1/2 cup julienned carrots

1/2 cup sliced red bell peppers

1/2 cup diced green onions

3 cups spaghetti sauce

1 teaspoon garlic powder

1 teaspoon McKay's Vegan Chicken Style Seasoning

1 teaspoon all-purpose salt-free seasoning

1/4 cup mild salsa

1/2 cup steamed broccoli flowerets

1/4 cup fresh chives

1/2 cup fresh parsley

Yield: 15 1/2-cup servings

Serving: Cal. 77   Fat 2.3g   Sat. fat <1g   Sod. 309.7mg   Carb. 11.9g   Diet. fiber 1g   Sugars 5.5g   Prot. 2.4g

Greek Florentine Fettuccine

1/2 pound uncooked fettuccine

1 medium onion, minced

3 cloves garlic, minced

1 tablespoon olive oil

2 cups canned diced tomatoes

2 tablespoons lemon juice

1 cup vegetable broth

1 teaspoon salt

1 teaspoon dried basil

1/2 teaspoon dried oregano

1 teaspoon dried parsley

1/2 teaspoon onion powder

1/2 teaspoon garlic powder

1 tablespoon McKay's Vegan Chicken Style Seasoning

5 cups chopped fresh spinach

1/2 cup grape tomatoes

1 cup sliced black olives

Cook pasta to al dente according to package directions. Drain and set aside.

While pasta is cooking, sauté onion and garlic in olive oil in a large skillet over medium heat until onion is clear. Add tomatoes, lemon juice, broth, and seasonings. Simmer for 15 to 20 minutes. Add fresh chopped spinach and cook for an additional five minutes. Add pasta, grape tomatoes, and black olives. Stir and serve hot!

My husband loves pasta so I am always trying new pasta dishes for him. This one has become a favorite. You can substitute frozen spinach for the fresh but I think fresh is the best. Also, if you like things a bit spicy, try adding 1/2 teaspoon cayenne pepper or 1/2 teaspoon crushed red pepper. —Brenda

Yield: 16 1/2-cup servings

Serving: Cal. 90 Fat 2.4g Sat. fat <1g Sod. 595.7mg Carb. 13.7g Diet. fiber 1.2g Sugars 1.8g Prot. 4g

Mushroom Stroganoff

In a skillet over medium heat, simmer onions and mushrooms in olive oil and salt until tender. Reduce heat to low, add the gluten and simmer an additional 5 to 10 minutes. Meanwhile, pour the soy milk into a medium-size pan and heat over medium-high heat. Add the Tofutti Better Than Sour Cream and seasonings. Mix the cornstarch with the cold water and, just before the sauce comes to a boil, slowly pour into the soy milk stirring until it thickens. Add the mushrooms, onions, and gluten pieces. Fold in the diced pimentos and angel hair pasta. Mix until well blended and pour onto serving platter. Garnish with fresh parsley and a grape tomato.

This makes a quick and easy meal and can be served right away or made the day before and baked right before serving at 350 degrees just until it is hot and bubbly. Serve with a fresh garden salad with lots of colorful vegetables, steamed broccoli, homemade wheat bread, and your favorite strawberry pie. Remember everyday to color your plate like a rainbow! Now enjoy all the wonderful things God has made for you! —Linda

2 tablespoons olive oil
1 cup diced fine onions
2 1/2 cups chopped fresh mushrooms
1/2 teaspoon salt
1 cup chopped gluten
4 cups soy milk
1 cup Tofutti Better Than Sour Cream
1 teaspoon all-purpose no-salt seasoning
1 teaspoon onion powder
1 teaspoon seasoned salt
1 teaspoon McKay's Vegan Chicken Style Seasoning
6 tablespoons cornstarch
6 tablespoons cold water
1/4 cup diced pimento
6 cups cooked angel hair pasta
2 sprigs fresh parsley
1 grape tomato

Yield: 24 1/2-cup servings

Serving: Cal. 125   Fat 3.9g   Sat. fat 2g   Sod. 100.5mg   Carb. 16.9g   Diet. fiber 1g   Sugars 1.6g   Prot. 5g

Zesty Spaghetti Sauce

2 to 3 cloves garlic,
    minced

1 medium onion,
    finely diced

1 tablespoon olive oil

2 cups chopped or
    sliced fresh
    mushrooms

1 medium red sweet
    pepper, chopped

2 cups finely chopped
    celery

1 12-ounce package
    Yves Veggie
    Ground Round
    or 2 cups
    vegetarian burger

2 15-ounce cans
    tomato sauce

1 tablespoon Italian
    seasoning

1 teaspoon garlic
    powder

1 to 2 teaspoons Pure
    Florida Crystals

In a large skillet over medium heat, sauté garlic and onion in olive oil until clear. Add mushrooms, pepper, and celery, and continue to sauté till tender. Add Veggie Ground Round stirring until completely heated. Add remaining ingredients. Simmer approximately 30 minutes. Serve hot over pasta of choice. Yields enough sauce for 1 pound uncooked (8 cups cooked) pasta.

I like to use this sauce for lasagna as well as other pasta. The Yves burger gives this sauce the texture of a hamburger sauce, so if you have a meat lover, this might just fool them! —Brenda

Yield: 16 1/2-cup servings

Serving: Cal. 58   Fat 1g   Sat. fat <1g   Sod. 20.6mg   Carb. 7.1g   Diet. fiber 1.7g   Sugars 3.6g   Prot. 4g

Spaghetti

In a medium-size saucepan combine the tomato sauce and seasonings and simmer. In a nonstick skillet over medium heat sauté the diced onions in olive oil until they are clear. Add the vegetarian burger and fry for an additional 5 to 10 minutes. Add the onions and burger to the sauce and simmer for 20 to 25 minutes to blend flavors.

Cook angel hair pasta according to package directions. Avoid overcooking. Remove from heat and drain. If the angel hair pasta is sticky, I either rinse it in a colander under warm water or add a little olive oil. Serve the pasta in a colorful bowl, pour the sauce into another bowl, and it is ready to eat.

This is a great recipe for those times when you need a fast and easy meal. You can even use the spaghetti sauce without simmering and it is still good. Just add a fresh green salad with lots of good raw vegetables, some homemade garlic bread, and Applesauce Carrot Cake (Cooking With the Micheff Sisters, p. 98). I love to invite the Lord's presence with us and then I know we will have a great time fellowshipping together. —Linda

5 cups tomato sauce

2 teaspoons Italian seasoning

2 teaspoons all-purpose no-salt seasoning

1/2 teaspoon salt

2 teaspoons garlic powder

1 teaspoon onion powder

1 cup finely chopped onion

2 tablespoons olive oil

2 cups Vibrant Life Vege-Burger

12 ounces angel hair pasta

Yield: 16 servings

Serving: Cal. 159   Fat 2.3g   Sat. fat <1g   Sod. 89.2mg   Carb. 22.2g   Diet. fiber 2.3g   Sugars 3.8g   Prot. 10.3g

Capellini Pomodoro

1 16-ounce package
angel hair
(capellini) pasta

3 tablespoons
+ 1 tablespoon
extra-virgin olive
oil

3 fresh garlic cloves,
minced

1/2 teaspoon crushed
dried red pepper

6 cups grape tomatoes
cut in thirds or
diced Roma
tomatoes

1 cup coarsely
chopped
fresh basil

2 tablespoons chopped
parsley

Cook pasta according to package directions. Drain the cooked pasta but do not rinse. Put into large serving bowl. In a large saucepan, heat 3 tablespoons olive oil and add the garlic and crushed red pepper. Sauté for 1 to 2 minutes. Add the tomatoes, basil, and parsley. Cook over medium heat for 3 to 5 minutes. Pour over the pasta and drizzle with the remaining 1 tablespoon of olive oil. Toss together and garnish with additional fresh basil.

This is perhaps my favorite of all Italian pasta dishes. The simplicity and fresh ingredients make it a summertime favorite. While my family and I were visiting in Italy I would order this at every restaurant we went to! This dish is one that should be made right before serving as the pasta will absorb all the liquid if it is made ahead and refrigerated. —Cinda

Yield: 24 1/2-cup servings

Serving: Cal. 103   Fat 2.8g   Sat. fat <1g   Sod. 5.5mg   Carb. 16.7g   Diet. fiber 1.4g   Sugars <1g   Prot. 3g

Fiesta Pasta & Rice

Heat olive oil in a large saucepan. Add pasta and rice and sauté on low heat until lightly browned. Add the water, salt, and salsa and mix well. Cover pan and cook 15 to 20 minutes. Remove cover and continue cooking for 5 more minutes, stirring occasionally. Serve hot.

This recipe is great for potlucks or picnics because it is also delicious at room temperature. It makes a wonderful accompaniment when I am serving haystacks in the park! You can make it the day before and transfer right to your picnic basket or cooler. It does not need to be reheated. —Cinda

- 2 tablespoons olive oil
- 1 pound angel hair pasta, broken into thirds
- 1 1/2 cups white or brown rice
- 4 cups water
- 2 teaspoons salt
- 3 cups salsa

Yield: 24 1/2-cup servings

Serving: Cal. 130 Fat 1.8g Sat. fat <1g Sod. 280.6mg Carb. 24.7g Diet. fiber 1.5g Sugars <1g Prot. 3.7g

Korean Chop Chay

1 tablespoon
+ 1 tablespoon
peanut oil

1 medium onion,
sliced in thin
slivers

2 cups thinly slivered
celery

3 cups sliced
mushrooms

6 cups thinly slivered
cabbage

3 cups julienned
carrots

4 ounces bean threads

1 cup Bragg Liquid
Aminos

Boiling water

1 tablespoon sesame
oil

In a wok or large skillet, sauté the onions, celery, and mushrooms in 1 tablespoon peanut oil. When tender, transfer to large bowl. (The celery should be slightly crunchy.) In 1 tablespoon peanut oil, sauté cabbage and carrots and cook until slightly tender. Add to bowl.

In a medium bowl, place raw bean threads and cover with boiling water. Pour Liquid Aminos over threads. Do not cook! Cover tightly and let sit for 8 to 10 minutes. Drain. With kitchen scissors make several cuts through the bean threads and then add to the vegetables. Toss with sesame oil until mixed well. Serve hot or at room temperature.

Our friends, the Kims, made something similar to this and brought it to church potlucks at our dad's church in Mineral Wells, Texas. We loved it so much that our mom asked for the recipe. Over the years, I have made it for my family but have altered the original recipe. I love the taste that the peanut oil gives and adding the sesame oil gives it a great toasty flavor! I have used this recipe to make spring rolls, called Cha Gio Chay. Take spring-roll wrappers, use this recipe as the filling, roll, and either fry or bake. They are delicious too! You can make this dish several days ahead of time but I don't recommend freezing it. —Brenda

Yield: 14 cups

Serving: Cal. 85   Fat 3.1g   Sat. fat <1g   Sod. 40.7mg   Carb. 14.6g   Diet. fiber 2.2g   Sugars 3.5g   Prot. 3.4g

Thai Noodles

Bring a large saucepan of lightly salted water to a boil. Add the snow peas and cook for 1 minute. With a slotted spoon remove peas to a colander and rinse under cold water. Put the Chinese noodles in the boiling water and cook according to the package directions. Drain but do not rinse. In a large serving bowl, combine the noodles, snow peas, shredded cabbage, carrots, cucumber, and sprouts. Stir in dressing and mix well. Sprinkle ground peanuts on top and serve at room temperature.

For dressing: In a glass measuring cup, make dressing by mixing together the peanut butter, water, lime juice, sesame oil, Liquid Aminos, sugar, salt, and red pepper flakes. Set aside.

I think the reason that I like Thai food so much is that they use peanuts in a lot of their dishes. And peanuts happen to be my very favorite of all the nuts! The different textures and flavors in this dish blend together beautifully. You can serve it with brown rice. I also like to eat it cold as a salad. —Cinda

Dressing
   (recipe below)

2 cups snow peas cut
   into thirds,
   strings removed

1 10-ounce package
   Chinese noodles

8 cups shredded
   cabbage

2 cups grated carrots

3 pickling cucumbers,
   peeled & diced

1 cup mung bean
   sprouts

1 cup finely chopped
   or ground
   peanuts

DRESSING

1/2 cup natural
   peanut butter

3 tablespoons water

2 tablespoons fresh
   lime juice

1 tablespoon dark
   sesame oil

1 tablespoon Bragg
   Liquid Aminos

1 teaspoon sugar

1 teaspoon salt

1 1/2 teaspoons
   crushed red
   pepper flakes

Yield: 18 1/2-cup servings

Serving: Cal. 210   Fat 13.4g   Sat. fat 2.1g   Sod. 506.6mg   Carb. 19.4g   Diet. fiber 3.8g   Sugars 5g   Prot. 6.5g

Pancit

1/2 pound rice sticks

1 cup thinly sliced carrots

1 cup thinly sliced celery

1 onion, diced (optional)

1/2 cup water

1 tablespoon McKay's Vegan Beef Style Seasoning

1 cup chopped gluten

1 package frozen whole green beans

2 to 4 tablespoons Bragg Liquid Aminos

1/2 teaspoon salt

1/4 teaspoon paprika

1 tablespoon Vege-Sal or other all-vegetable seasoning

1 tablespoon dark sesame oil

Soak rice sticks in hot water for about 20 minutes. Drain. Sauté the carrots, celery, and onion, if using, in water. Sprinkle Beef Style Seasoning over vegetables. Add gluten and green beans and sauté until green beans are tender. Add rice sticks, Liquid Aminos, and seasonings and continue cooking over medium heat for about 15 minutes. Sprinkle with dark sesame oil and mix. Place in serving dish and garnish as desired.

This is one of my daughter Catie's favorite dishes. She even likes it cold! I buy canned oriental vegetarian gluten and use that in this dish. You can purchase it at any oriental food market and some grocery stores will carry it. It really has a great flavor and truly enhances this dish. I also use my homemade gluten and that tastes good too. —Cinda

Yield: 20 1/2-cup servings

Serving: Cal. 69   Fat <1g   Sat. fat <1g   Sod. 138.8mg   Carb. 12.6g   Diet. fiber <1g   Sugars <1g   Prot. 2.7g

Pizza & Calzones

Indian Summer
Pizza
p. 123

Tostada Pizza
p. 116

**Mushroom Spinach
Calzones
p. 131**

**Rosemary Chicken
Potato Pizza
p. 125**

Tostada Pizza

1 pound Honey Wheat
Pizza Dough
(recipe on p. 135)

2 cups mild salsa

2 cups drained, rinsed
black beans

2 cups drained, rinsed
pinto beans

3 cups shredded lettuce

2 cups chopped
tomatoes

1/4 cup sliced olives

1/2 cup chopped
avocado

1 cup baked tortilla
strips

Tofu Ranch Dressing
(recipe below)

TOFU RANCH DRESSING

1 12.3-ounce package
Mori-Nu Silken
Soft Tofu

1/4 cup Vegenaise

1/4 cup cold water

1 teaspoon McKay's
Vegan Chicken
Style Seasoning

1 teaspoon onion
powder

1/2 teaspoon garlic
powder

1/4 cup Tofutti Sour
Supreme

1/2 teaspoon lemon
juice

1 teaspoon parsley

Stretch pizza dough on a 14-inch pizza pan that has been sprayed with nonstick vegetable spray. Spread salsa on top of the dough with a rubber spatula. Cover the top of the salsa with the black beans and pinto beans. Bake at 350 degrees for 20 to 30 minutes until bottom of crust is golden brown. Remove from oven and top with lettuce, tomato, olives, avocado, and chips. Drizzle Tofu Ranch Dressing on top and garnish with a spoonful of salsa in the middle.

This is one of my favorite pizzas. I made this one at 3ABN and served it to some of the employees and they loved it. Top off the meal with fresh fruit and homemade cookies. Enjoy! —Linda

For Tofu Ranch Dressing: Put all the ingredients except parsley in the blender and blend until smooth, then stir in parsley. Chill until ready to serve.

This dressing will keep in the refrigerator for a couple of weeks. I have used this dressing as a substitute for mayo. It also makes a great sandwich spread and a wonderful dressing for taco salad or tossed vegetable salad. —Linda

Yield: 12 3 1/3-inch slices; 40 tablespoons dressing

Per slice: Cal. 136   Fat 2.5g   Sat. fat <1g   Sod. 277.3mg   Carb. 22.9g   Diet. fiber 5.9g   Sugars 2.6g   Prot. 6.4g
Per tablespoon dressing: Cal. 6   Fat <1g   Sat. fat <1g   Sod. 58mg   Carb. <1g   Diet. fiber <1g   Sugars <1g   Prot. <1g

Eggplant Pizza

Wash the eggplant and cut it into thin slices leaving the skins on. Put the slices in a large bowl of cold water with 1 teaspoon salt. Set aside for 5 to 10 minutes.

Put the sliced onions and soy margarine into a glass bowl with lid. Microwave for 5 to 6 minutes until onions are tender. Take the eggplant slices and dip them one at a time in the seasoned flour mixture. Spread 2 tablespoons of olive oil on a baking pan and place the eggplant on the pan. Slices should be touching. Place them as close together as you can as they do shrink while baking. Spray the tops of the eggplant with vegetable nonstick cooking spray. Bake at 350 degrees for 20 to 30 minutes until lightly browned on one side. You do not need to bake slices on both sides.

To assemble your pizza stretch the pizza dough on a 14-inch pizza pan sprayed with nonstick vegetable spray. Spread 1/2 the spaghetti sauce on top of the dough and sprinkle with garlic powder. Cover the sauce with 1/2 the eggplant. Spread the remaining spaghetti sauce on top. Sprinkle garlic powder on top of sauce. Place the rest of the eggplant on top of the sauce. (There should be two layers of sauce and eggplant ending with the eggplant on top.) Bake at 350 degrees for 20 to 25 minutes until crust is golden brown.

For seasoned flour: Mix all ingredients together in a large bowl.

Sometimes I sauté peppers and zucchini and sprinkle them on top of the pizza along with sliced olives. My husband is not an eggplant fan but he loves this pizza! And eggplant is so good for us! Purple vegetables like eggplant are rich sources of anthocyanins and phenois. Both of these phytochemicals are powerful antioxidants that can help reduce the risk of cancer, heart disease, and Alzheimer's. So enjoy your meal with this healthy pizza! —Linda

Yield: 12 3 1/3-inch slices

---

1 large eggplant, thinly sliced

1 teaspoon salt

1 large onion, sliced

1 tablespoon soy margarine

Seasoned flour (recipe below)

2 tablespoons olive oil

1 pound Honey Wheat Pizza Dough (recipe on p. 135)

1 26-ounce can spaghetti sauce

1 teaspoon garlic powder

SEASONED FLOUR

1 cup white wheat flour

1/2 cup brewers yeast flakes

1 tablespoon McKay's Vegan Beef Style Seasoning

1 tablespoon McKay's Vegan Chicken Style Seasoning

1 tablespoon Vege-Sal

1/2 teaspoon onion powder

1/4 teaspoon garlic powder

Per slice: Cal. 112   Fat 1.4g   Sat. fat <1g   Sod. 771.8mg   Carb. 20.7g   Diet. fiber 4.6g   Sugars 5.4g   Prot. 4.6g

Vege-Sausage Pizza

1 pound Honey Wheat Pizza Dough (recipe on p. 135)

1 to 2 cups spaghetti sauce

1 medium red bell pepper, thinly sliced

1 medium yellow bell pepper, thinly sliced

1 sweet onion, thinly sliced

2 to 3 cups vegan sausage

1/2 cup sliced olives

Stretch pizza dough on a 14-inch pizza pan that has been sprayed with a nonstick cooking spray. Spread spaghetti sauce on top of the dough with a rubber spatula. Cover the sauce with the peppers and onions and top with the sausage pieces and olives. Bake pizza at 350 degrees for 20 to 25 minutes until crust is golden brown.

This pizza can be made up ahead and frozen before it is baked. Then when friends drop in for a visit just pull the pizza out of the freezer, pop it in the oven, and the delicious smells of a home-baked meal will make any guest feel welcomed. My mom taught us the importance of always being ready for extra people at mealtime. Dad and Mom believed in opening up their hearts and home to all. I've tucked those happy memories in my heart and now I too love opening up my home to others! And planning ahead helps to make this a stress-free enjoyable time for all. —Linda

Yield: 12 3 1/2-inch slices

Per slice: Cal. 84   Fat 3.9g   Sat. fat <1g   Sod. 286.4mg   Carb. 7g   Diet. fiber 2.2g   Sugars 3g   Prot. 5.5g

Mini-Meatball Pizza

Gently stretch the dough until it covers a large baking tray with 1-inch high sides. Spread the spaghetti sauce over the dough. Sprinkle the garlic powder on top of the sauce. Spread the mini-meatballs over the top of the sauce. Sprinkle the onions and olives on top of the meatballs. Bake at 350 degrees for 25 to 30 minutes or until the crust is golden brown.

For mini-meatballs: In the blender put the tofu, onion, Beef Style Seasoning, garlic powder, and Liquid Aminos. Blend until smooth. Pour the blended tofu and seasonings into a medium-size bowl. Stir in the pecan meal and cracker crumbs. Shape the mixture, 1 teaspoon at a time, into 100 mini-meatballs. Spray a cookie sheet with vegetable nonstick cooking spray and place the meatballs on the tray. Spray the top of the meatballs with vegetable nonstick cooking spray and bake at 350 degrees for 20 to 25 minutes or until golden brown. Take out of oven and set aside.

The mini-meatballs can be made ahead and frozen up to a couple of months. I like to make up a double batch of these meatballs so I have extra to serve at another meal with sweet and sour sauce. With life so full and busy this really helps me put a nutritious meal together quickly when I am blessed with drop-in guests. I'm so glad that God is always prepared for our drop-in visits too! —Linda

1 pound pizza dough
3 cups spaghetti sauce
1/2 teaspoon garlic powder
Mini-meatballs (recipe below)
2 cups sliced onions
1 cup sliced olives

MINI-MEATBALLS

1 12.3-ounce package Mori-Nu Silken Tofu
1 medium onion
1 teaspoon McKay's Vegan Beef Style Seasoning
1/4 teaspoon garlic powder
1 tablespoon Bragg Liquid Aminos
1 cup pecan meal
2 cups crushed saltine crackers or breadcrumbs

Yield: 24 3 1/2-inch squares

Per square: Cal. 90   Fat 2.2g   Sat. fat <1g   Sod. 293.6mg   Carb. 12.7g   Diet. fiber 1g   Sugars 2.8g   Prot. 5.1g

Black Bean & Salsa Pizza

1 medium onion, cut
   in slivers

1 tablespoon extra-
   virgin olive oil

1 pound pizza dough

1 1/2 cups mild salsa

1 red bell pepper, cut
   in small strips

1 cup halved grape
   tomatoes

1 cup sliced black
   olives

1 cup drained, rinsed
   black beans

Diced jalapeños
   to taste

In a medium skillet over medium heat sauté the onion slivers in the olive oil until clear. Stretch your favorite pizza dough over a 14-inch pizza pan. Spread salsa over the dough. Place bell pepper, tomatoes, olives, black beans, and jalapeños evenly over the dough. Bake at 400 degrees for 15 to 20 minutes until the bottom of pizza crust is golden.

This is one of my favorite pizzas! I love using the salsa instead of the traditional pizza sauce; it gives it a zesty southwestern flavor. —Cinda

Yield: 12 3 1/2-inch slices

Per slice: Cal. 59   Fat 2.9g   Sat. fat <1g   Sod. 210.5mg   Carb. 7.3g   Diet. fiber 1.8g   Sugars <1g   Prot. 1.9g

Wild West Chili Pizza

In a large saucepan, heat the oil and add the onion. Sauté on medium heat until the onion is clear. Add the garlic, cumin, and chili powder. Sauté another 2 minutes and then add the tomato sauce, salsa, and the beans. (It is not necessary to rinse the beans.) Stir well, remove from heat, and set aside. Spray a 14-inch round pizza pan with a nonstick cooking spray. Spread the corn bread batter evenly over the pan. Bake at 400 degrees for 8 minutes. Remove from oven and spread the chili mixture over the top. Sprinkle the frozen corn and the chopped red pepper over the top. Return to oven and bake another 10 minutes until crust is golden brown on the bottom.

This recipe is fun to make in smaller individual pizzas. I provide lots of extra toppings and let each person create their own unique pizza. I add plenty of chopped jalapeño peppers to mine! You just might want to invite some friends over to try this recipe with you! —Cinda

1 medium onion, chopped

2 tablespoons canola or olive oil

1 tablespoon minced garlic

2 teaspoons cumin

2 teaspoons chili powder

3 tablespoons mild or medium salsa

1 8-ounce can tomato sauce

1 15-ounce can dark red kidney beans, drained

1 15-ounce can pinto beans, drained

3 cups corn bread batter (recipe on p. 137)

1/2 cup frozen sweet corn

1 medium red bell pepper, seeded and chopped

Yield: 12 3 1/2-inch slices

Per slice: Cal. 136 Fat 2.9g Sat. fat <1g Sod. 28.9mg Carb. 21.1g Diet. fiber 6.2g Sugars 1.4g Prot. 6.9g

Red Pepper & Black Bean Pizza

1 pound Honey Wheat
 Pizza Dough
 (recipe on p. 135)

1 tablespoon cornmeal

1 to 2 cups pizza
 sauce

2 cups drained, rinsed
 black beans

1 1/2 cup whole
 kernel sweet corn

1/2 cup diced green
 chiles

1 to 2 tablespoons
 diced jalapeño
 peppers
 (optional)

1 cup roasted
 red peppers
 (recipe below)

ROASTED RED PEPPERS

3 to 4 red bell peppers

1 to 2 tablespoons
 olive oil

Stretch pizza dough on a 14-inch pizza pan that has been sprinkled with cornmeal. Spread pizza sauce on top of dough with a rubber spatula. Sprinkle beans, corn, chiles, jalapeños if using, and red peppers evenly on dough. Bake at 400 degrees 15 to 20 minutes until bottom of crust is golden. Remove from oven and serve immediately.

For roasted red peppers: Spread olive oil on a cookie sheet. Slice peppers into thin strips. Place on oiled cookie sheet and bake at 400 degrees until peppers are soft and slightly dark on edges.

I like things on the spicy side so I use the jalapeños and sometimes even double the amount, but I usually just put them on half the pizza. That way everyone is happy! I especially like the flavor of the wheat crust with this pizza. White bread just doesn't have enough nutrients in it to satisfy me!
—Brenda

Yield: 12 3 1/2-inch slices

Per slice: Cal. 115   Fat 3.4g   Sat. fat <1g   Sod. 255.5mg   Carb. 19g   Diet. fiber 4g   Sugars 2.9g   Prot. 4.3g

Indian Summer Pizza

In medium skillet sauté onion slivers in olive oil until almost clear. Add peppers and mushrooms and cook until slightly tender. Set aside. Sprinkle the cornmeal on a 14-inch pizza pan. Stretch pizza dough on pan and top with spaghetti sauce. Sprinkle onions, pepper, and mushroom mixture evenly across entire pizza. Top with chili beans, green chilies, and corn. Bake at 400 degrees for 15 to 20 minutes until bottom of crust is golden. Serve hot or at room temperature.

Sometimes I like to spice this up with sliced jalapeños, but if you don't like it so spicy use mild chili beans. For a stronger onion taste, omit sautéing the onions, peppers, and mushrooms and use raw. I personally don't like the flavor of raw onions so I always sauté them. —Brenda

1 medium onion, sliced in thin slivers

2 tablespoons olive oil

1 medium yellow or red bell pepper, sliced in thin slivers

3 cups sliced mushrooms (optional)

1 tablespoon cornmeal

1 pound Honey Wheat Pizza Dough (recipe on p. 135)

1 cup spaghetti sauce

1 cup hot chili beans

1/2 cup green chiles

1 cup corn

Yield: 12 3 1/2-inch slices

Per slice: Cal. 79 Fat 3.1g Sat. fat <1g Sod. 315.1mg Carb. 11.7g Diet. fiber 2.2g Sugars 2.4g Prot. 2.7g

Vegetable Pizza

1 medium eggplant

1 cup soy milk

2 to 3 cups seasoned
breadcrumbs

1 tablespoon cornmeal

1 pound Honey Wheat
Pizza Dough
(recipe on p. 135)

1 cup spaghetti sauce

1 cup chopped
spinach

1 medium onion,
slivered

2 cups broccoli florets

3 cups sliced
mushrooms

Wash and slice eggplant into about 30 1/2-inch rounds. Dredge eggplant slices in soy milk. Cover each side in breadcrumbs. Place on baking sheet that has been sprayed with a nonstick cooking spray. Bake at 375 for 30 to 40 minutes until golden. Set aside.

Sprinkle the cornmeal on a 14-inch pizza pan. Stretch pizza dough on pan. Spread spaghetti sauce over dough. Layer the spinach, onions, broccoli, mushrooms, and baked eggplant slices on entire pizza, in that order. Bake at 400 degrees for 15 to 20 minutes until bottom of crust is golden. Serve hot or at room temperature.

I use cornmeal on the bottom of the crust to prevent sticking but you can use a nonstick cooking spray in place of the cornmeal if preferred. Be aware that the bottom crust will be crisper if using the nonstick cooking spray. Sometimes I try different vegetables such as corn, peas, and even potatoes! Experiment with your favorite vegetables on pizza. Yummy! —Brenda

Yield: 12 3 1/2-inch slices

Per slice: Cal. 143   Fat 2.2g   Sat. fat <1g   Sod. 550.1mg   Carb. 25.4g   Diet. fiber 3.8g   Sugars 4.7g   Prot. 6.1g

Rosemary Chicken-Potato Pizza

Peel and slice potatoes in circles approx 1/8-inch thick. Place the slices on a cookie sheet sprayed with nonstick cooking spray and bake in oven at 375 degrees until slices are easily pierced with a fork. Remove from oven and set aside.

In a mixing bowl, place 2 cups of boiling water and Chicken Style Seasoning. Add Soy Add-ums. Stir and let stand for 30 minutes and then drain, squeezing out excess liquid.

Sprinkle a 14-inch pizza pan with cornmeal. Stretch out pizza dough to cover pan. Spread olive oil and lemon juice on top of dough with a rubber spatula. Sprinkle on the finely minced garlic. Next sprinkle on the Soy Add-ums. Layer potato slices overlapping in a circular pattern, until entire pizza is covered. Drizzle with melted margarine or olive oil. Sprinkle with rosemary and parsley and salt to taste. Bake in a 400 degree oven 15 to 20 minutes until bottom of crust is golden.

A pizza similar to this was a favorite of mine in a restaurant in Boston, although I would order it without the chicken. When I moved to Knoxville, I decided to make this at home. I experimented with Soy Add-ums and am very happy with how they work because they absorb the chicken flavoring and have a meatlike texture. Don't get carried away on the rosemary though, because a little goes a long way! —Brenda

3 to 4 medium-large potatoes

2 tablespoons McKay's Vegan Chicken Style Seasoning

1 cup Soy Add-ums

1 pound Honey Wheat Pizza Dough (recipe on p. 135)

1 tablespoon cornmeal

1 tablespoon olive oil

1 tablespoon fresh lemon juice

1 to 2 cloves garlic, finely minced

1/2 teaspoon rosemary

1 teaspoon dried parsley

2 tablespoons margarine, melted

Salt to taste

Yield: 12 3 1/2-inch slices

Per slice: Cal. 98   Fat 3.1g   Sat. fat <1g   Sod. 296.9mg   Carb. 15.4g   Diet. fiber 2.3g   Sugars <1g   Prot. 3g

BLT Pizza

1 pound pizza dough

1 tablespoon
    cornmeal

1 to 2 tablespoons
    olive oil

10 to 12
    Worthington
    Stripples or other
    imitation bacon
    strips

2 to 3 tablespoons
    grapeseed oil
    Vegenaise

1 tablespoon
    soy milk

3 to 4 cups chilled
    chopped lettuce

3 to 4 medium
    tomatoes,
    chopped or sliced

Stretch your favorite pizza dough over a 14-inch pizza pan that has been sprinkled with cornmeal. Spread olive oil on top of dough with a rubber spatula. Cut Stripples into 1-inch pieces and sprinkle on top of pizza. Bake in a 400 degree oven 15 to 20 minutes until bottom of crust is golden. While pizza is baking, mix together Vegenaise and soy milk until smooth. Remove pizza from oven when finished baking. Toss the chilled chopped lettuce with the Vegenaise mixture and spread on the pizza. Top with the chopped or sliced tomatoes. Serve immediately.

This tastes very much like a veggie bacon, lettuce, and tomato sandwich! You can bake the pizza ahead of time and set aside. Top with the Vegenaise, lettuce, and tomatoes right before serving. Sometimes I like to add black olives for variety! —Brenda

Yield: 12 3 1/2-inch slices

Per slice: Cal. 220   Fat 11g   Sat. fat 1g   Sod. 262.1mg   Carb. 27.5g   Diet. fiber 3.7g   Sugars 4.5g   Prot. 5g

Blueberry-Apple Crumb *Pizza*

In a medium saucepan heat apple-juice concentrate and 1/2 teaspoon cinnamon over medium heat until it comes to a boil. In a separate container mix cornstarch and cold water. Stirring constantly with a wire whisk, pour cornstarch slowly into the hot apple-juice concentrate. Set aside to cool.

In a mixing bowl, place flour, brown sugar, and 1/2 teaspoon cinnamon. Cut margarine into flour mixture, forming fine pieces to make a crumb topping. Set aside. Sprinkle a 14-inch pizza pan with cornmeal and stretch the dough over it. Add apples and blueberries to apple juice mixture and fold until well mixed. Spread over pizza dough. Top with crumb topping. Bake in a 400 degree oven 15 to 20 minutes until bottom of crust is golden and apples are tender. Serve hot or cold.

For variety, add 1 cup quick oats to crumb mixture. You can also substitute walnuts and raisins for the blueberries. —Brenda

1 12-ounce can apple-juice concentrate, undiluted

1/2 teaspoon + 1/2 teaspoon cinnamon

2 to 3 tablespoons cornstarch

1/4 cup cold water

1 cup unbleached flour

1 cup brown sugar

6 tablespoons margarine

1 tablespoon cornmeal

1 pound Honey Wheat Pizza Dough (recipe on p. 135)

5 to 6 medium Granny Smith or Cortland apples, thinly sliced

1 cup fresh or frozen blueberries

Yield: 8 6-inch calzones

Per calzone: Cal. 273   Fat 6.1g   Sat. fat 1g   Sod. 83.8mg   Carb. 54.7g   Diet. fiber 2.5g   Sugars 26.1g   Prot. 1.7g

Breakfast Calzones

1 cup finely diced onion

2 tablespoons extra-virgin olive oil

2 cups coarsely chopped fresh mushrooms

3 medium potatoes, peeled, diced, & cooked

2 cups chopped fresh spinach

2 tablespoons McKay's Vegan Chicken Style Seasoning

1 teaspoon Vege-Sal or all-purpose seasoning

2 packages firm or extra firm tofu or 3 cups water packed tofu cut into 1/2-inch cubes

1 pound pizza dough

In a large nonstick skillet, sauté the onion in olive oil until tender and clear in color.

Add the mushrooms, potatoes, spinach, Chicken Style Seasoning, and Vege-Sal. Mix until everything is well blended.

Drain the tofu and cut into 1/2-inch cubes and add to the rest of the ingredients. Continue to sauté for 5 to 10 minutes until mixture is hot and mushrooms are tender. Remove from heat and set aside.

Divide the prepared dough into 8 4-ounce balls and cover with a towel. Let rise for about 5 minutes. Roll each ball out into 8-inch circles. Place 1/2 cup of the topping mixture on the bottom half of each circle, leaving about an inch all the way around. Fold the top half of the circle over the filling and crimp the edges to seal them. Spray a baking sheet with a nonstick vegetable spray, and carefully transfer the calzones to the baking sheet. Lightly brush the tops of the calzones with extra-virgin olive oil. Make a small hole or slit in the top of each one to allow the steam to escape. Bake in a 400 degree oven for 15 to 20 minutes until the top and bottom of the calzones are golden brown. Remove from oven and allow to cool for 5 minutes before serving.

This mixture can also be spread on the top of a single pizza crust and baked. It is delicious both ways. I love to serve this for a special brunch as well as for breakfast. You can make the mixture up to two days ahead of time and refrigerate until ready to place into the pizza dough and bake. —Cinda

Yield: 8 6-inch calzones

Per calzone: Cal. 183   Fat 5.9g   Sat. fat <1g   Sod. 461.8mg   Carb. 24.5g   Diet. fiber 2.2g   Sugars 2.1g   Prot. 8.4g

Spinach-Cheese Calzones

Put the spinach, salt, and seasoned salt in a large skillet over medium heat. Cook until spinach is thawed and tender. Add the Better Than Cream Cheese and stir until it has melted and blended into the spinach. Remove from heat and set aside while making the dough.

Divide the prepared dough into 8 4-ounce balls and cover with a towel. Let rise for about 5 minutes. Roll each ball out into 8-inch circles. Place 1/2 cup of the topping mixture on the bottom half of each circle, leaving about an inch all the way around. Fold the top half of the circle over the filling and crimp the edges to seal them. Spray a baking sheet with a nonstick vegetable spray, and carefully transfer the calzones to the baking sheet. Lightly brush the tops of the calzones with extra-virgin olive oil. Make a small slit in the top of each one to allow the steam to escape. Bake in a 400 degree oven for 15 to 20 minutes until the top and bottom of the calzones are golden brown. Remove from oven and allow to cool for 5 minutes before serving. Serve hot or cold.

These calzones are a wonderful way to entice your kids to eat spinach. Serve the calzones with a colorful vegetable salad and a luscious dish of watermelon and cantaloupe.

Some of my fondest memories as a child were of helping Mom make delicious meals out of bread dough. The price for this special bonding time is only the cost of the meal! When the kids are grown the times spent in the kitchen creating family meals will be a wonderful memories, turning their hearts toward home. —Linda

8 cups frozen chopped spinach, thawed & squeezed dry

1 teaspoon salt

1 teaspoon seasoned salt

8 ounces French onion flavor Better Than Cream Cheese

Calzone dough (recipe on p. 133)

Yield: 16 6-inch calzones

Per calzone: Cal. 58 Fat 3.7g Sat. fat <1g Sod. 325.5mg Carb. 4.5g Diet. fiber 2.4g Sugars <1g Prot. 3.6g

Potato-Onion Calzones

8 cups diced potatoes,
   cooked &
   drained

1 cup diced onions,
   cooked

8 ounces Better Than
   Cream Cheese

1 tablespoon soy
   margarine,
   melted

1 tablespoon onion
   powder

5 teaspoons seasoned
   salt

2 pounds calzone
   dough
   (recipe on p. 133)

In a large bowl, whip the potatoes, onions, Better Than Cream Cheese, soy margarine, onion powder, and seasoned salt until well blended.

Divide the prepared dough into 16 4-ounce balls and cover with a towel. Let rise for about 5 minutes. Roll each ball out into 6-inch circles. Place 1/2 cup of the topping mixture on the bottom half of each circle, leaving about an inch all the way around. Fold the top half of the circle over the filling and crimp the edges to seal them. Spray a baking sheet with a nonstick vegetable spray, and carefully transfer the calzones to the baking sheet. Lightly brush the tops of the calzones with extra-virgin olive oil. Make a small slit in the top of each one to allow the steam to escape. Bake in a 400 degree oven for 15 to 20 minutes until the top and bottom of the calzones are golden brown. Remove from oven and allow to cool for 5 minutes before serving.

The Potato-Onion Calzones are great served with a colorful vegetable tray and fresh fruit salad. For our meal, I like to make a couple of different kinds of calzones. Sandwich spreads make great fillings. Whatever filling you make, be sure and add an extra amount of love. Then your family is sure to enjoy your special meal! —Linda

Yield: 16 6-inch calzones

Per calzone: Cal. 208   Fat 4g   Sat. fat <1g   Sod. 144mg   Carb. 39.6g   Diet. fiber 3.7g   Sugars <1g   Prot. 4.4g

Mushroom-Spinach Calzones

In a large skillet over medium heat, add water and Chicken Style Seasoning. Cook until onion is clear. Add the mushrooms and continue to cook until the mushrooms are tender. In a separate container mix the Wondra flour and soy milk together until well blended. Pour into the ingredients in the skillet. Add the Vege-Sal, oregano, salt if using, and the spinach. Stir until well mixed and remove from the heat.

Divide the prepared dough into 8 4-ounce balls and cover with a towel. Let rise for about 5 minutes. Roll each ball out into 8-inch circles. Place 1/2 cup of the topping mixture on the bottom half of each circle, leaving about an inch all the way around. Fold the top half of the circle over the filling and crimp the edges to seal them. Spray a baking sheet with a nonstick vegetable spray, and carefully transfer the calzones to the baking sheet. Lightly brush the tops of the calzones with extra-virgin olive oil. Make a small slit in the top of each one to allow the steam to escape. Bake in a 400 degree oven for 15 to 20 minutes until the top and bottom of the calzones are golden brown. Remove from oven and allow to cool for 5 minutes before serving.

You may use whatever mushrooms are plentiful and available in your area. I like to use more than one variety to add flavor to the filling. You can use frozen spinach if you thaw it completely and squeeze all the juice out. Spinach is one of those green and leafy vegetables that are so good for us. While you are enjoying the taste of these calzones, your body is benefiting from the vitamins and minerals the spinach is supplying. Enjoy! —Cinda

1 cup water

1 small onion, chopped

1 tablespoon McKay's Vegan Chicken Style Seasoning

2 cups sliced baby portobello mushrooms

2 cups sliced button or shiitake mushrooms

1/2 cup Wondra flour

2 cups soy milk

3 tablespoons Tofutti Sour Cream

1 teaspoon Vege-Sal or all-purpose seasoning

3/4 teaspoon oregano

Salt to taste

4 cups coarsely chopped fresh spinach

1 pound pizza dough

Yield: 8 6-inch calzones

Per calzone: Cal. 82 Fat 1.4g Sat. fat <1g Sod. 248.1mg Carb. 13.8g Diet. fiber 2.7g Sugars 2g Prot. 5.4g

Sloppy Joe Calzones

2 tablespoons canola or olive oil

1 cup chopped onions

2 cups chopped celery

2 cups vegetarian burger

3 tablespoons Pure Florida Crystals

2 tablespoons lemon juice

2 tablespoons Bragg Liquid Aminos

2 tablespoons vegetarian Worcestershire sauce

1 1/2 cups fruit sweetened ketchup

1 6-ounce can tomato paste

1 1/2 pounds pizza or bread dough

Heat the oil in a large skillet over medium heat. Add the chopped onion and celery and sauté until onion is clear. Add the vegetarian burger and continue to sauté for a couple of minutes. Add remaining ingredients except dough. Mix well. Simmer on low heat for 30 minutes.

Divide the prepared dough into 8 4-ounce balls and cover with a towel. Let rise for about 5 minutes. Roll each ball out into 8-inch circles. Place 1/2 cup of the topping mixture on the bottom half of each circle, leaving about an inch all the way around. Fold the top half of the circle over the filling and crimp the edges to seal them. Spray a baking sheet with a nonstick vegetable spray, and carefully transfer the calzones to the baking sheet. Lightly brush the tops of the calzones with extra-virgin olive oil. Make a small slit in the top of each one to allow the steam to escape. Bake in a 400 degree oven for 15 to 20 minutes until the top and bottom of the calzones are golden brown. Remove from oven and allow to cool for 5 minutes before serving.

This recipe is very similar to the one my mom made when we were kids. She let her filling simmer for 2 hours! The flavor certainly does get richer and better the longer you let it simmer. When I let mine simmer longer, it always makes me smile. The rich aroma fills the kitchen and reminds me of my childhood! You can also serve this on warm hamburger buns. —Cinda

Yield: 12 6-inch calzones

Serving: Cal. 100 Fat 2.4g Sat. fat <1g Sod. 64.4mg Carb. 10.1g Diet. fiber 1.8g Sugars 6g Prot. 7.1g

Calzone Dough

In a large mixing bowl put the water, oil, salt, honey, 2 cups of the whole-wheat flour, and the active dry yeast. Whip together for about 5 minutes. Slowly add the rest of the flour to form soft dough. Knead the dough for 5 to 10 minutes. Spray the bottom of the bowl with nonstick vegetable spray and cover the dough with a clean cloth. Let the dough rise about 20 minutes until double in size. Divide the dough into 16 4-ounce balls. Roll into 8-inch circles and place your favorite filling on half of the dough leaving an inch all the way around for sealing. Fold the top half of the dough on top of the filling and roll the ends up to the filling. Crimp the ends as you would a piecrust. Place on a greased tray and let the dough rest for about 10 minutes. Bake at 350 degrees for 20 to 25 minutes or until calzones are golden brown. Serve hot or cold.

This calzone dough can be used to make pizza crust, dinner rolls, or bread. The fragrance that comes from my oven and fills my house reminds me that God blesses our efforts to make our homes special. I always smile when I hear my husband say, "Wow, it smells so good in here." I find it is really the little things in life that make for a happy home. Try making some homemade bread and watch your family smile! —Linda

2 cups warm water
1/2 cup canola oil
2 teaspoons salt
1/4 cup honey
2 tablespoons active dry yeast
5 cups white wheat flour
2 tablespoons vital wheat gluten

Yield: 16 8-inch calzone crusts

Per crust: Cal. 214   Fat 7.5g   Sat. fat <1g   Sod. 293.7mg   Carb. 33.2g   Diet. fiber 3.5g   Sugars 4.4g   Prot. 5.3g

Thin & Crispy Pizza Crust

2 cups warm water
1 teaspoon active dry yeast
3 cups all-purpose flour
3 cups whole-wheat flour
1 teaspoon salt
4 tablespoons cornmeal

Mix this dough by hand. In a large bowl dissolve the yeast in the water. In another large bowl, combine flour and the salt and mix well. Add 3 cups of flour to the yeast and mix thoroughly. While stirring with a spoon, slowly add the rest of the flour until dough becomes thick enough to knead with your hands. Continue kneading until the dough is smooth and elastic and not sticky. Cover with a light towel and let rise 15 minutes. Divide dough into fourths. Spray a 12-inch pizza pan with a nonstick cooking spray. Sprinkle pan with 1 tablespoon of the cornmeal. With your hands, work one of the sections of dough into a large circle. Place the circle on the pan and spread dough out to completely cover it. Crust should be approximately 1/4-inch thick. Bake the crust at 425 degrees for 10 minutes. Remove and cover with desired toppings. Return to oven and bake for 15 to 20 minutes until the bottom is golden brown and crispy.

I learned this recipe from my brother Kenny's wife, Tammy. It is not only fat free, but delicious! I like the flavor that the whole-wheat flour adds. You can make up the crusts ahead of time and freeze until ready to use. My son David usually brings 15 to 20 college kids home with him on the weekends. On Saturday nights I like to make small individual pizzas and let each one put their own toppings on. All the kids enjoy creating their own culinary masterpieces. —Cinda

Yield: 4 12-inch pizza crusts

Per crust: Cal. 704   Fat 3.5g   Sat. fat <1g   Sod. 591.2mg   Carb. 147.6g   Diet. fiber 15.1g   Sugars <1g   Prot. 23.8g

Honey Wheat Pizza Dough

In a large mixing bowl, place water, oil, salt, honey, oatmeal, molasses, and white flour. Mix together and then add yeast. Gradually add wheat flour until a thick dough is formed. Place dough on floured countertop and knead 10 to 15 minutes until smooth and elastic. Spray the mixing bowl with a nonstick spray and place dough in bowl. Cover and let rise in a warm place 20 to 30 minutes until double in size. Punch dough down and let rise again. When dough has doubled again, punch it down and divide into 6 equal parts. Stretch dough onto a round 14-inch pizza pan that has been sprinkled with cornmeal. Cover with pizza sauce and toppings and bake in a 400 degree oven for 15 to 20 minutes until bottom of crust is golden. Serve hot!

You can freeze the pizza dough on the pizza pan until ready for use. Let thaw at room temperature before baking. If you like a lighter crust, use more white flour than wheat. This makes wonderful bread and dinner rolls too!
—Brenda

4 cups very warm water
2/3 cup canola oil
1 tablespoon salt
2/3 cup honey
1 cup cooked oatmeal
1/2 cup molasses
4 cups white wheat flour
4 tablespoons active dry yeast
5 to 8 cups whole-wheat flour

Yield: 6 14-inch pizza crusts

Per crust: Cal. 1192   Fat 28.2g   Sat. fat 2.4g   Sod. 1246mg   Carb. 213.7g   Diet. fiber 21.9g   Sugars 38.4g   Prot. 32g

Pizza Dough

1 cup water

1/4 cup canola oil

1 teaspoon salt

2 tablespoons honey

1 cup + 3/4 cup whole-wheat flour

1 tablespoon active dry yeast

1 cup white wheat flour

1 tablespoon vital wheat gluten

In a large bowl put the water, oil, salt, honey, 1 cup wheat flour, and the active dry yeast. Mix together and whip for about 5 minutes. Slowly add the rest of the flour until it becomes soft dough. Knead for 5 to 10 minutes. Spray the bottom and sides of the bowl with vegetable spray and cover the dough with a clean towel. Let the dough rise until double in size. Spray a 14-inch pizza pan with vegetable spray and stretch the dough in place. Put the sauce and toppings on and bake at 350 degrees for 25 to 30 minutes or until bottom of crust is golden brown.

The homey smells of pizza baking in the oven bring back so many treasured childhood memories. On Sundays Dad would organize a big ball game at our house with the young people in the church and Mom would make homemade pizza. It was their way of making others feel welcomed in our home. Now that I am older, I too love sharing the blessings of my home with others. Make an extra pizza and invite someone over . . . and share God's blessings! —Linda

Yield: 1 14-inch pizza crust

Crust: Cal. 1812   Fat 60.2g   Sat. fat 4.8g   Sod. 2351mg   Carb. 287g   Diet. fiber 31.6g   Sugars 34.8g   Prot. 46.4g

Grandma's Corn Bread

In a medium-size bowl mix all the dry ingredients together. Make a well in the middle of the dry ingredients and add all the liquid ingredients. Mix together until blended. Pour into an 8-inch square pan that has been sprayed with nonstick vegetable spray. Bake at 350 degrees for about 25 minutes. Serve hot.

This recipe will make 12 regular size or 24 mini cornbread muffins. It can be used as a topping for casseroles or a pizza crust as well. —Linda

1 cup yellow cornmeal

1 cup unbleached flour

1 tablespoon baking powder

1/2 teaspoon salt

1 cup soy milk

1/4 cup pure maple syrup

1/4 cup canola oil

Yield: 12 2 x 2 2/3-inch pieces

Per piece: Cal. 180 Fat 6.2g Sat. fat <1g Sod. 110.8mg Carb. 27.8g Diet. fiber 2.4g Sugars 4.4g Prot. 3.9g

Resources

DRESSLERS: Soy Good milk and Soy Add-ums and other wonderful healthy products.

Dressler Foods, Inc.
184 Panorama Lane
Walla Walla, WA 99362
888-526-6330
www.dresslerfoods.com

COUNTRY LIFE NATURAL FOODS: They offer a line of natural, whole, and organic foods at reasonable prices. They carry most of the specialty items in this cookbook, such as white-wheat flour, Mori-Nu Tofu, Mori-Nu Mates, kelp, McKay's Vegan Chicken and Beef Style Seasoning, Bragg Liquid Aminos, Vegex, pure maple syrup, whole grains, herbs, spices, and over 1,200 other natural items. To order, call 1-800-456-7694, and they will ship directly to your house by UPS. Ask for their free catalog.

TOFUTTI: Manufactures a variety of nondairy items that are soy based and casein-free: Sour Supreme, Better Than Cream Cheese, various soy cheeses, and much more.

Tofutti Brands, Inc.
50 Jackson Drive
Cranford, NJ 07016
908-272-2400 or 908-272-9492
www.tofutti.com

MORI-NU: They have a variety of products that we use; most common is their tofu. It does not have to be refrigerated, which makes it wonderful to stock. You can purchase it in many grocery stores as well as natural food stores.

Morinaga Nutritional Foods, Inc.
2441 West 205th Street, Suite C102
Torrance, CA 90501
Phone: 310-787-0200 | Fax: 310-787-2727
www.morinu.com

FOLLOW YOUR HEART: They are the makers of Grapeseed Oil Vegenaise and the original Vegenaise. In our opinion, these vegan "mayonnaise" products are the best on the market.

Follow Your Heart Natural Foods
P.O. Box 9400
Canoga Park, CA 91309-0400
Phone: 818-725-2820
Fax: 818-725-2812
www.followyourheart.com

LIBERTY RICHTER COMPANY: They manufacture a soy milk that we love called Better Than Milk. It is available in natural food stores and Adventist Book Centers, and they also ship this product all over the world.

Liberty Richter
400 Lyster Ave.
Saddle Brook, NJ 07663
Phone: 800-494-8839 or 201-843-8900
www.libertyrichter.com

YVES VEGGIE CUISINE: They produce healthy vegetarian soy meat substitutes that are not only packed with nutrition and flavor but low in fat and calories! One of the things we love best is the texture, and also that it doesn't have an overwhelming flavor. It takes on whatever flavor you give it and no aftertaste that is common in other products!

1-800-434-4246

www.yvesveggie.com

DISMAT CORPORATION: McKay's Vegan Chicken or Beef Style Seasoning

Dismat Corporation
336 N. Westwood Avenue
Toledo, OH 43607

Phone: 419-531-8963 | Fax: 419-531-8965
Email: mckayssoupmix@bex.net

VIBRANT LIFE FOODS: They have a wide variety of nutritious soy and gluten meat substitutes, such as Vegeburger, Vege-Franks, and Vege-Scallops, just to name a few. Their products are available at many grocery and natural food stores and can also be ordered by contacting them at their toll free number.

Vibrant Life Foods
11145 Anderson Street, BC203
Loma Linda, CA 92350

Phone: 888-893-2002 | Fax: 909-558-0377
Email: llwf@llu.edu

www.vibrantlife.info

PACIFIC PRESS ABC CHRISTIAN BOOK CENTERS: They offer a wide variety of health books and vegetarian, vegan cookbooks.

800-765-6955

www.adventistbookcenter.com

THREE ANGELS BROADCASTING NETWORK (3ABN): This network is the second largest religious network in the world, and they offer a number of health programs. You will be able to view vegan cooking programs and receive additional recipes on 3ABN Television or 3ABN Radio which, broadcast 24 hours a day.

Three Angels Broadcasting
P.O. Box 220
West Frankfort, IL 62896

618-627-4651
Email: mail@3abn.org
www.3abn.org

Index

Measurements & Equivalents

3 teaspoons	= 1 tablespoon		1 teaspoon	= 5 milliliters
4 tablespoons	= 1/4 cup		1 tablespoon	= 15 milliliters
5 tablespoons + 1 teaspoon	= 1/3 cup		1 fluid ounce	= 30 milliliters
8 tablespoons	= 1/2 cup		2 fluid ounces	= 60 milliliters
12 tablespoons	= 3/4 cup		8 fluid ounces (1 cup)	= 240 milliliters
16 tablespoons	= 1 cup		16 fluid ounces (1 pint)	= 480 milliliters
1 tablespoon	= 1/2 fluid ounce		32 fluid ounces (1 quart)	= 950 milliliters
1 cup	= 8 fluid ounces		128 fluid ounces (1 gallon)	= 3.75 liters
2 cups	= 1 pint			
4 cups or 2 pints	= 1 quart			
4 quarts	= 1 gallon			

WEIGHT

Metric equivalents rounded

1/4 ounce	7 grams
1/2 ounce	14 grams
1 ounce	28 grams
4 ounces	115 grams
8 ounces (1/2 pound)	225 grams
16 ounces (1 pound)	455 grams
32 ounces (2 pounds)	910 grams
40 ounces (2 1/4 pounds)	1 kilogram

OVEN TEMPERATURE

Fahrenheit	Celsius	Gas Setting
275 degrees	140 degrees	Mark 1
300 degrees	150 degrees	Mark 2
325 degrees	160 degrees	Mark 3
350 degrees	180 degrees	Mark 4
375 degrees	190 degrees	Mark 5
400 degrees	200 degrees	Mark 6
425 degrees	220 degrees	Mark 7
450 degrees	230 degrees	Mark 8
475 degrees	240 degrees	Mark 9
Broil		Grill